BASS GUITAR
SONGS FOR KIDS

ISBN 978-1-7051-1108-6

HAL•LEONARD®

Visit Hal Leonard Online at
www.halleonard.com

Contact us:
Hal Leonard
7777 West Bluemound Road
Milwaukee, WI 53213
Email: info@halleonard.com

In Europe, contact:
Hal Leonard Europe Limited
42 Wigmore Street
Marylebone, London, W1U 2RN
Email: info@halleonardeurope.com

In Australia, contact:
Hal Leonard Australia Pty. Ltd.
4 Lentara Court
Cheltenham, Victoria, 3192 Australia
Email: info@halleonard.com.au

Bass Rhythm Tab Legend

Rhythm Tab is a form of notation that adds rhythmic values to the traditional tab staff.

TABLATURE graphically represents the bass guitar fingerboard. Each horizontal line represents a string, and each number represents a fret. Rhythmic values are shown using ovals, stems, and dots.

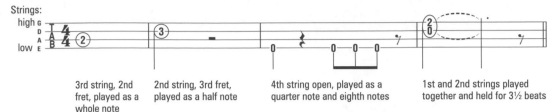

3rd string, 2nd fret, played as a whole note

2nd string, 3rd fret, played as a half note

4th string open, played as a quarter note and eighth notes

1st and 2nd strings played together and held for 3½ beats

Definitions for Special Notation

QUARTER-STEP BEND: Strike the note and bend up 1/4 step.

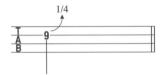

BEND AND RELEASE: Strike the note and bend up as indicated, then release back to the original note. Only the first note is struck.

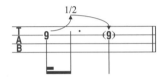

VIBRATO: The string is vibrated by rapidly bending and releasing the note with the fretting hand.

HAMMER-ON: Strike the first (lower) note with one finger, then sound the higher note (on the same string) with another finger by fretting it without picking.

PULL-OFF: Place both fingers on the notes to be sounded. Strike the first note, and without picking, pull the finger off to sound the second (lower) note.

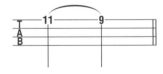

LEGATO SLIDE: Strike the first note and then slide the same fret-hand finger up or down to the second note. The second note is not struck.

SHIFT SLIDE: Same as legato slide, except the second note is struck.

GRACE-NOTE SLUR: Strike the note and immediately hammer-on (pull-off or slide) as indicated.

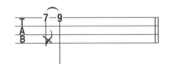

NATURAL HARMONIC: Strike the note while the fret hand lightly touches the string directly over the fret indicated.

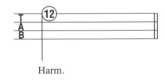

Harm.

MUTED STRING: A percussive sound is produced by laying the fret hand across the string without depressing, and striking it with the pick hand.

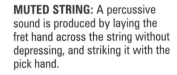

Additional Musical Definitions

  (staccato) • Play the note short

  (fermata) • A hold or pause

D.S. al Coda • Go back to the sign (%), then play until the measure marked *"To Coda,"* then skip to the section labelled *"Coda."*

D.C. al Fine • Go back to the beginning of the song and play until the measure marked *"Fine"* (end).

Bass Fig. • Label used to recall a recurring pattern.

N.C. • No chord

tacet • Instrument is silent (drops out).

• Repeat measures between signs

• When a repeated section has different endings, play the first ending only the first time and the second ending only the second time.

All About That Bass

Words and Music by Kevin Kadish and Meghan Trainor

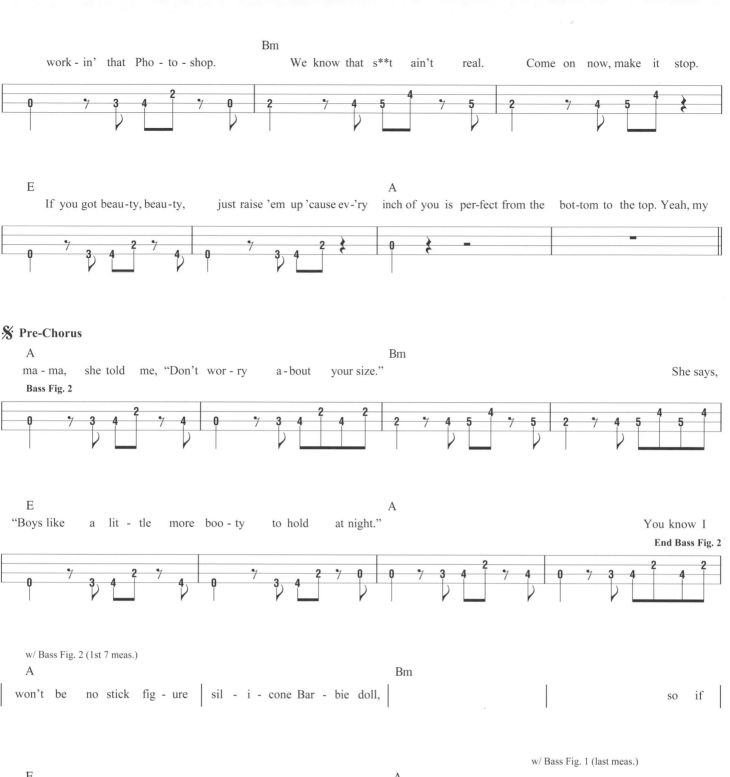

work - in' that Pho - to - shop.   We know that s**t ain't   real.   Come on now, make it   stop.

If you got beau - ty, beau - ty,   just raise 'em up 'cause ev - 'ry   inch of you is per - fect from the   bot - tom to the top. Yeah, my

Pre-Chorus

ma - ma,   she told   me, "Don't wor - ry   a - bout   your size."   She says,

Bass Fig. 2

"Boys like   a lit - tle   more boo - ty   to hold   at night."   You know I

End Bass Fig. 2

w/ Bass Fig. 2 (1st 7 meas.)

won't be   no stick fig - ure   sil - i - cone Bar - bie doll,   so if

w/ Bass Fig. 1 (last meas.)

that's what you're in - to then   go a - head   and move a - long.   Be - cause you know I'm

Chorus

w/ Bass Fig. 1

all a - bout that bass, 'bout that   bass, no tre - ble. I'm   all a - bout that bass, 'bout that   bass, no tre - ble. I'm

To Coda ⊕

all a - bout that bass, 'bout that   bass, no tre - ble. I'm   all a - bout that bass, 'bout that   bass, hey. 2. I'm bring - in'

Verse

A   N.C.   A   Bm

boo - ty back.   Go a - head and tell them skin - ny b***h - es that.

No, I'm just play-in', I know you   think you're fat,   but I'm here to tell you ev - 'ry

E

D.S. al Coda   ⊕ **Coda**

A

inch of you is per - fect from the   bot - tom to the top. Yeah, my   bass.   Be - cause you know I'm

w/ Bass Fig. 2

A

‖: all a - bout that bass, 'bout that | bass,   no   tre - ble.   I'm | all a - bout that bass, 'bout that |

Bm

bass,   no   tre - ble.   I'm | all a - bout that bass, 'bout that | bass,   no   tre - ble.   I'm |

E

1.   2.

A

| all a - bout that bass, 'bout that | bass.   Be - cause you know I'm :‖ bass, 'bout that bass, 'bout that ‖

Outro

w/ Bass Fig. 2 (1st 4 meas.)

A   Bm

| bass. Hey,   hey. | Hey, | hey.   Ooh, | you know you know this |

E   A

bass.   Hey.

All Star

Words and Music by Greg Camp

Tune down 1/2 step:
(low to high) Eb-Ab-Db-Gb

Key of G

Verse
Moderately

G	D	Am	C
1. Some - bod - y once told me the world	is gon - na roll me;	I

Bass Fig. 1 .... End Bass Fig. 1

w/ Bass Fig. 1 (3 times)

G	D	Am	C	G	D
ain't the sharp - est tool in the shed.		She was	look - ing kind of dumb with her fin -

Am	C	G	D	Am	C
- ger and her thumb in the shape	of an "L" on her fore	- head.	2. Well, the

Verse

w/ Bass Fig. 1 (3 times)

G	D	Am	C
years start com - ing and they don't stop com - ing.	Fed to the rules, and I hit the ground run - ning.

3. *See additional lyrics*

G	D	Am	C
Did - n't make sense not to live for fun. Your	brain gets smart, but your head gets dumb.

G	D	Am	C
So much to do, so much to see. So what's wrong	with tak - ing the back streets? You'll

G	D	Am	C	F
nev - er know if you don't go.	You'll nev - er shine if you don't glow.

Chorus

G	C	C#m7b5	C
Hey now, you're an all star;	get your game on, go play.

Bass Fig. 2 .... End Bass Fig. 2

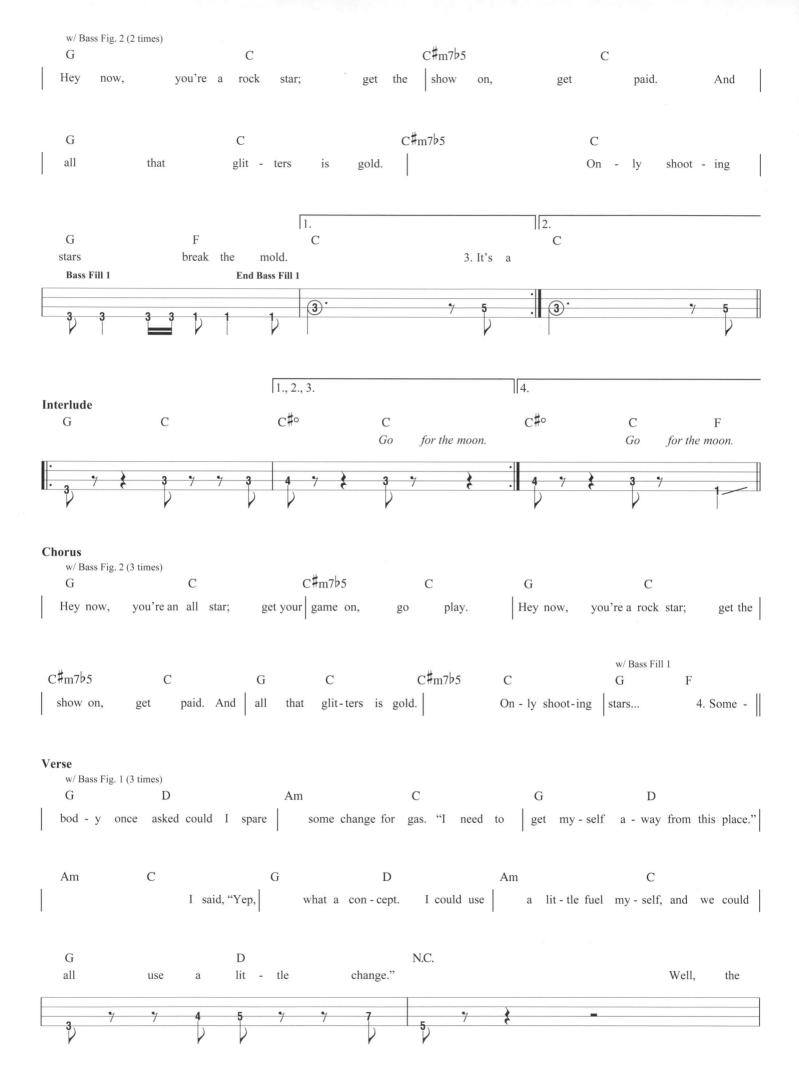

Additional Lyrics

3. It's a cool place, and they say it gets colder.
   You're bundled up now; wait till you get older.
   But the meteor men beg to differ,
   Judging by the hole in the satellite picture.
   The ice we skate is getting pretty thin.
   The water's getting warm so you might as well swim.
   My world's on fire. How 'bout yours?
   That's the way I like it and I'll never get bored.

Bad Day

Words and Music by Daniel Powter

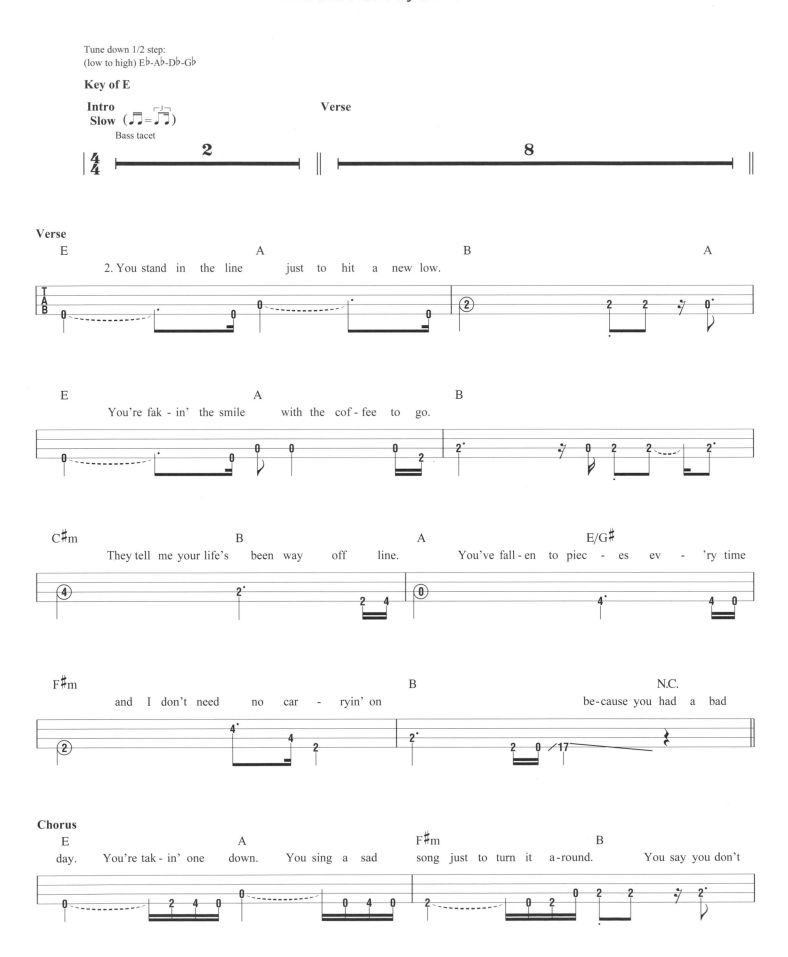

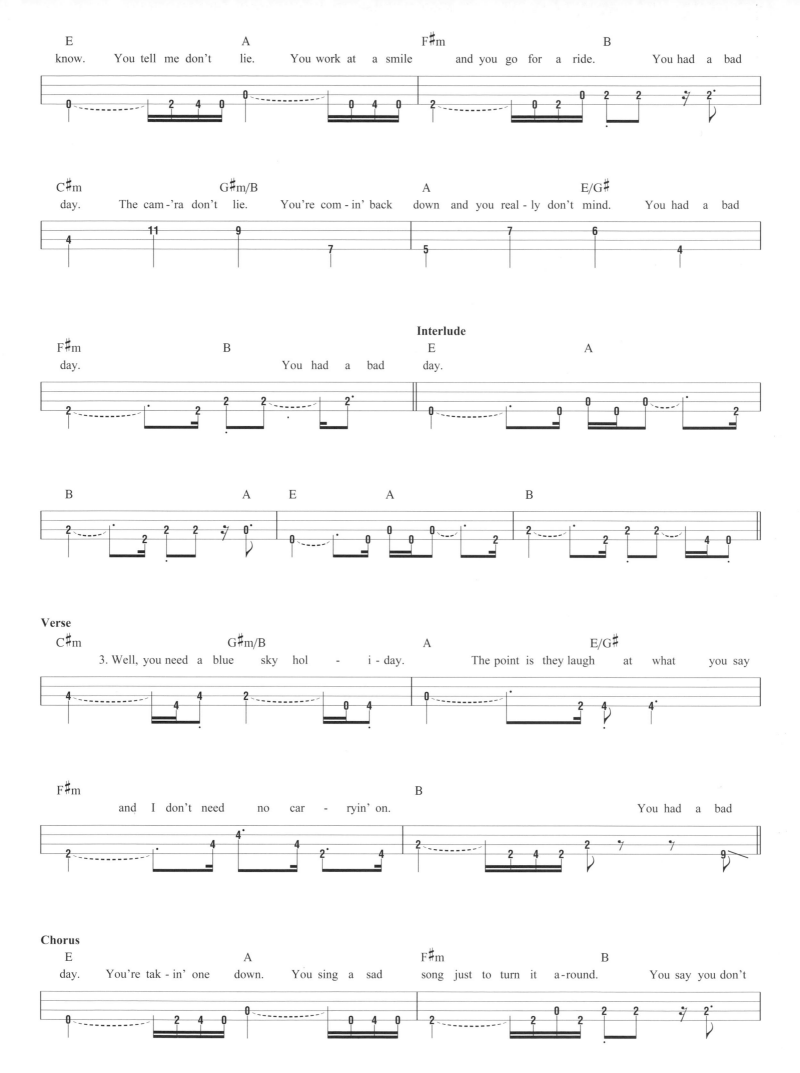

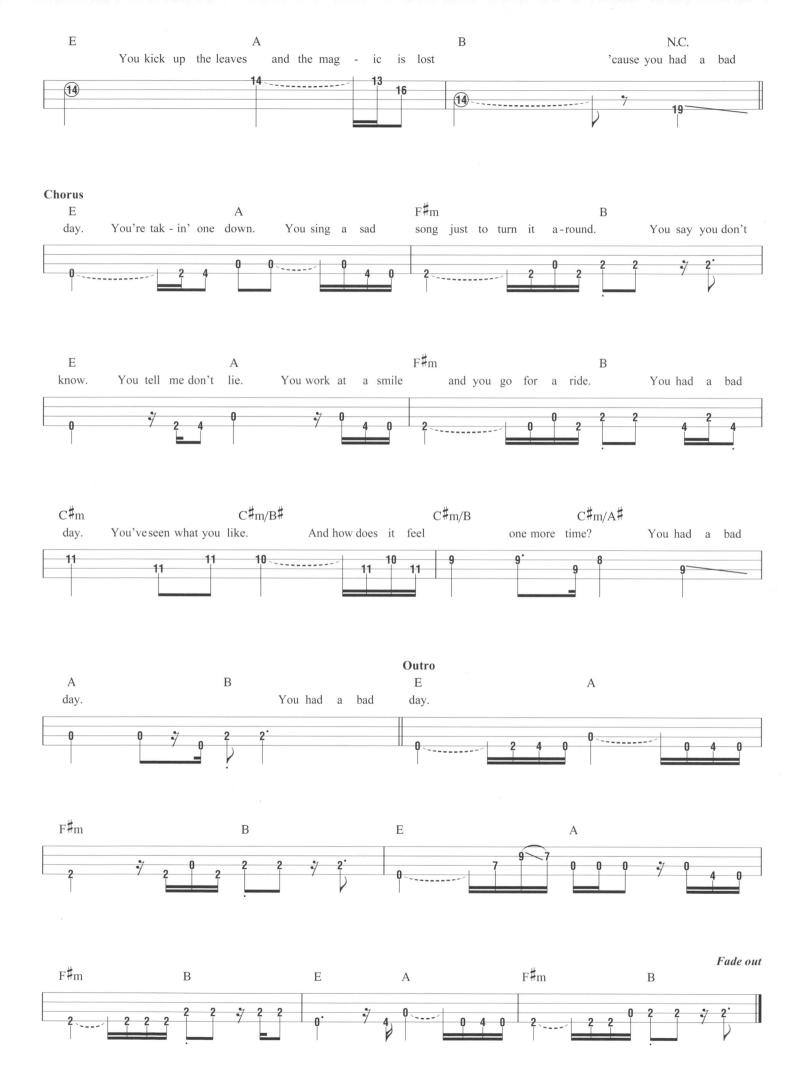

Best Day of My Life

Words and Music by Zachary Barnett, James Adam Shelley,
Matthew Sanchez, David Rublin, Shep Goodman and Aaron Accetta

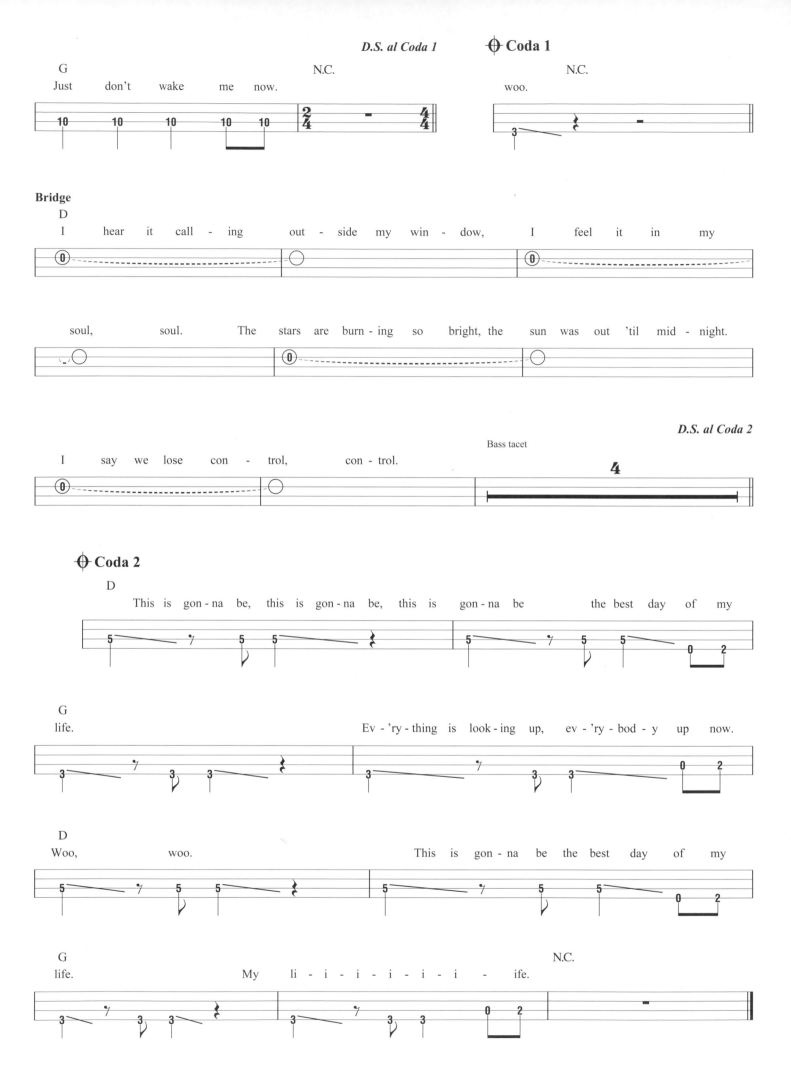

Can't Stop the Feeling!

from TROLLS

Words and Music by Justin Timberlake, Max Martin and Shellback

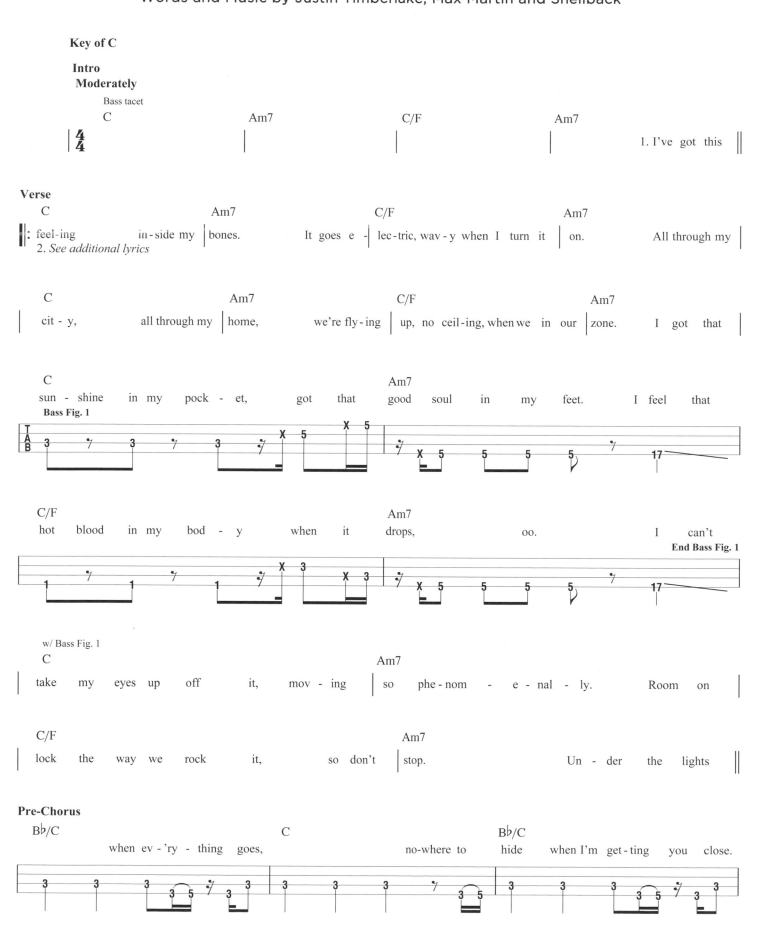

Key of C

Intro
Moderately

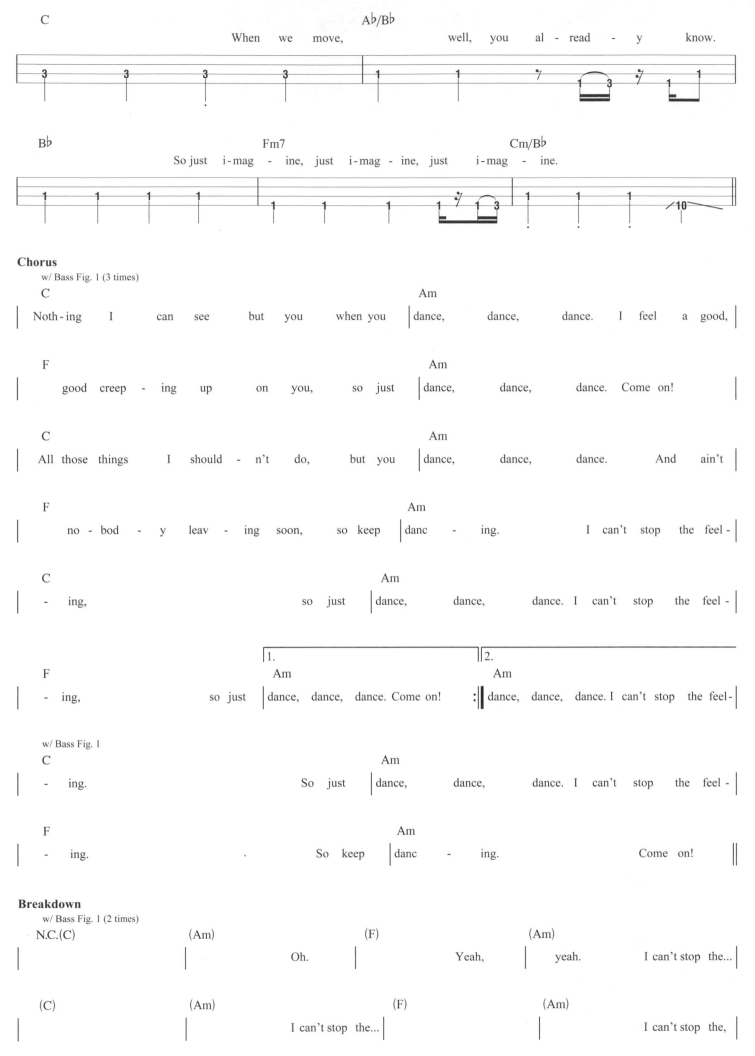

Chorus
w/ Bass Fig. 1 (3 times)

C ..... Am
Noth-ing I can see but you when you | dance, dance, dance. I feel a good,

F ..... Am
good creep-ing up on you, so just | dance, dance, dance. Come on!

C ..... Am
All those things I should-n't do, but you | dance, dance, dance. And ain't

F ..... Am
no-bod-y leav-ing soon, so keep | danc - ing. I can't stop the feel-

C ..... Am
- ing, so just | dance, dance, dance. I can't stop the feel-

1. ..... 2.
F ..... Am ..... Am
- ing, so just | dance, dance, dance. Come on! :|| dance, dance, dance. I can't stop the feel-

w/ Bass Fig. 1
C ..... Am
- ing. So just | dance, dance, dance. I can't stop the feel-

F ..... Am
- ing. So keep | danc - ing. Come on! ||

Breakdown
w/ Bass Fig. 1 (2 times)
N.C.(C) ..... (Am) ..... (F) ..... (Am)
| Oh. | Yeah, | yeah. I can't stop the...

(C) ..... (Am) ..... (F) ..... (Am)
| I can't stop the... | I can't stop the,

Bass tacet

w/ Bass Fig. 1 (4 times)

C

I can't stop the,   I can't stop the feel... ‖ Noth-ing I   can   see   but   you   when you

Am   F

dance,   dance,   dance. I feel a good, | good creep - ing up on you, so just

Am   C

dance,   dance,   dance. Come on! | All those things I should - n't do, but you

Am   F

dance,   dance,   dance. And ain't | no - bod - y leav - ing soon, so keep

Am   C

danc - ing.   I can't stop the feel | - ing. Got this feel - ing in my

Am   F

bod - y.   I can't stop the feel | - ing. Got this feel - ing in my

Am   C

bod - y.   I can't stop the feel | - ing. Wan - na see you move your

Am   F

bod - y.   I can't stop the feel | - ing. Got this feel - ing in my

Bass tacet

Am   N.C.

bod - y.   Break it | down! Got this feel - ing in my

bod - y.   Can't stop the feel | - ing. Got this feel - ing in my

bod - y.   Come on! |

Additional Lyrics

2. Ooh, it's something magical.
It's in the air, it's in my blood, it's rushing on.
I don't need no reason, don't need control.
I fly so high, no ceiling, when I'm in my zone.
'Cause I got that...

Call Me Maybe

Words and Music by Carly Rae Jepsen, Joshua Ramsay and Tavish Crowe

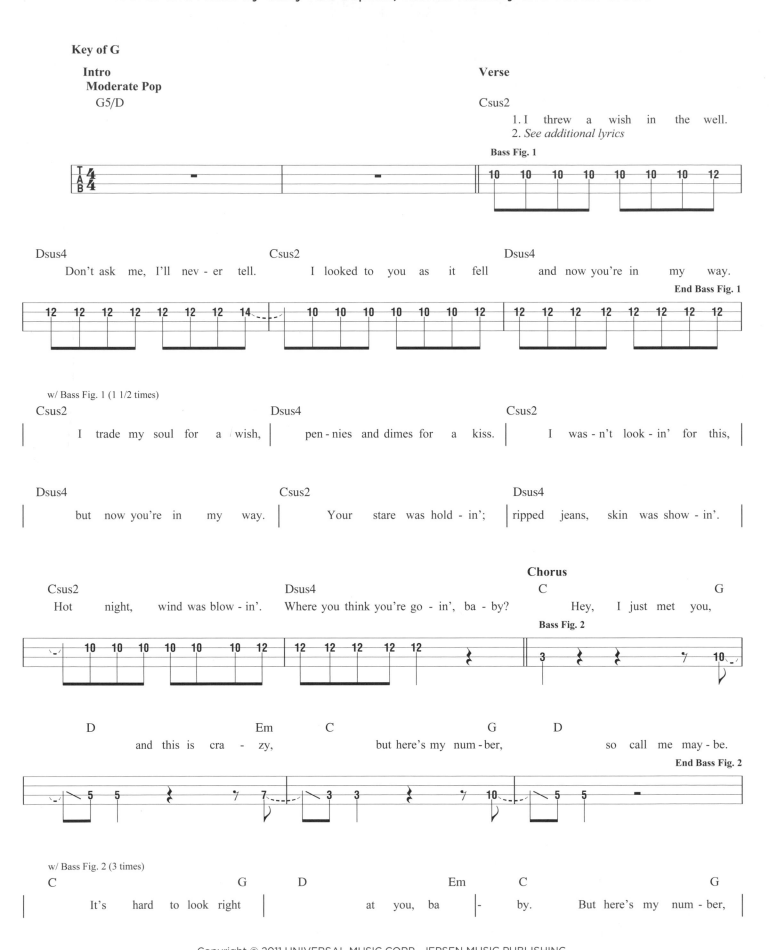

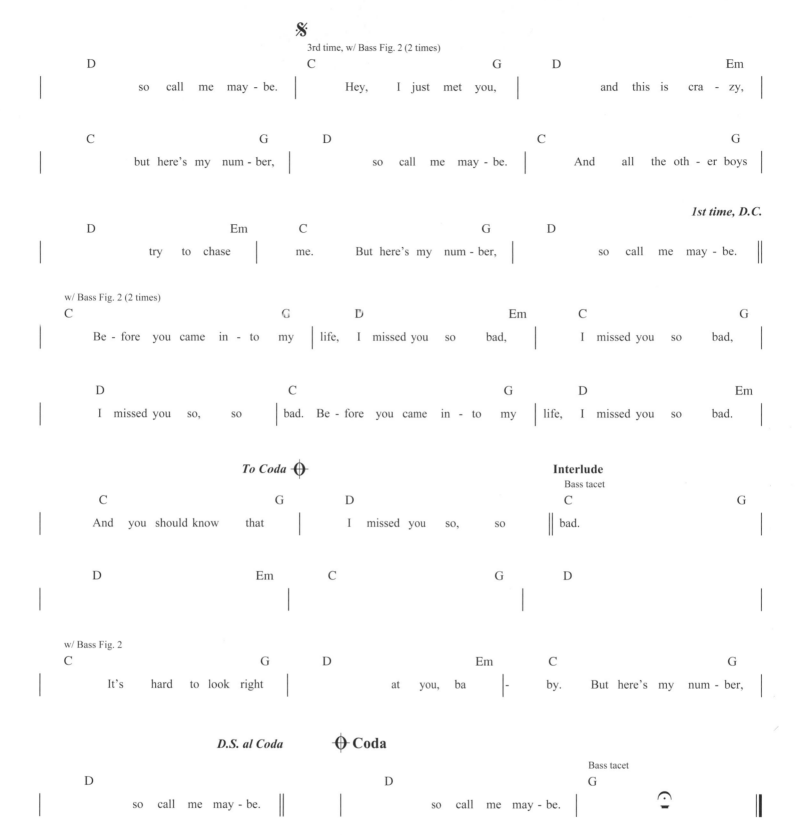

Additional Lyrics

2. You took your time with the call,
   I took no time with the fall.
   You gave me nothin' at all,
   But still you're in my way.
   I beg and borrow and steal,
   At first sight and it's real.
   I didn't know I would feel it,
   But it's in my way.
   Your stare...

Castle on the Hill

Words and Music by Ed Sheeran and Benjamin Levin

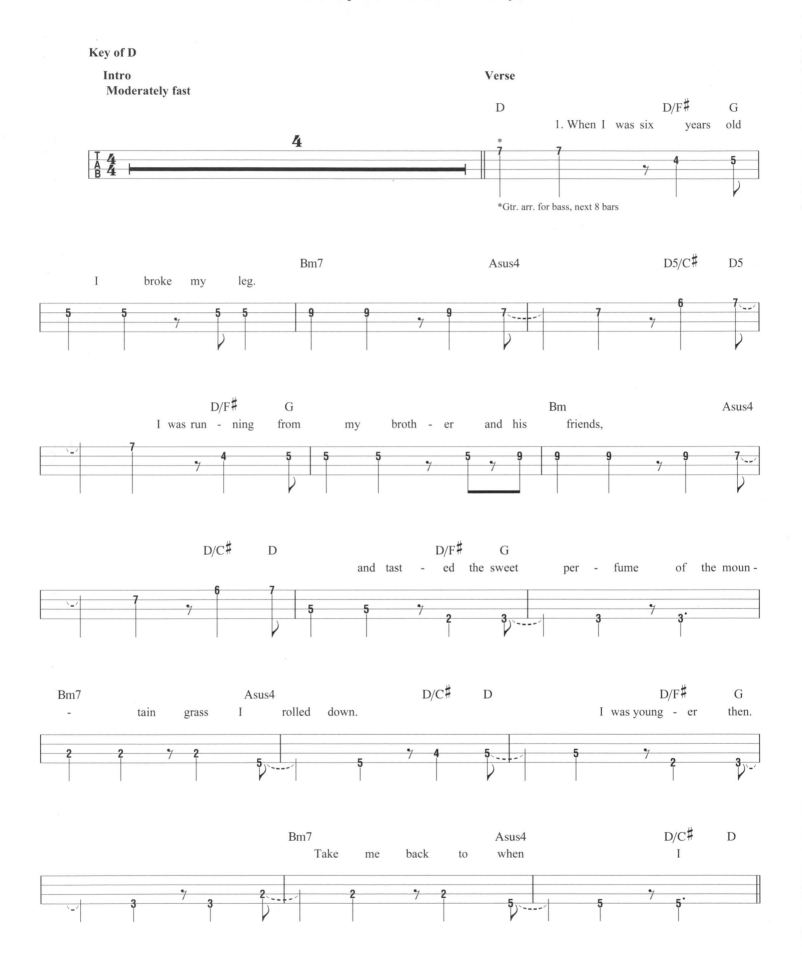

Interlude

To Coda 1
To Coda 2

24

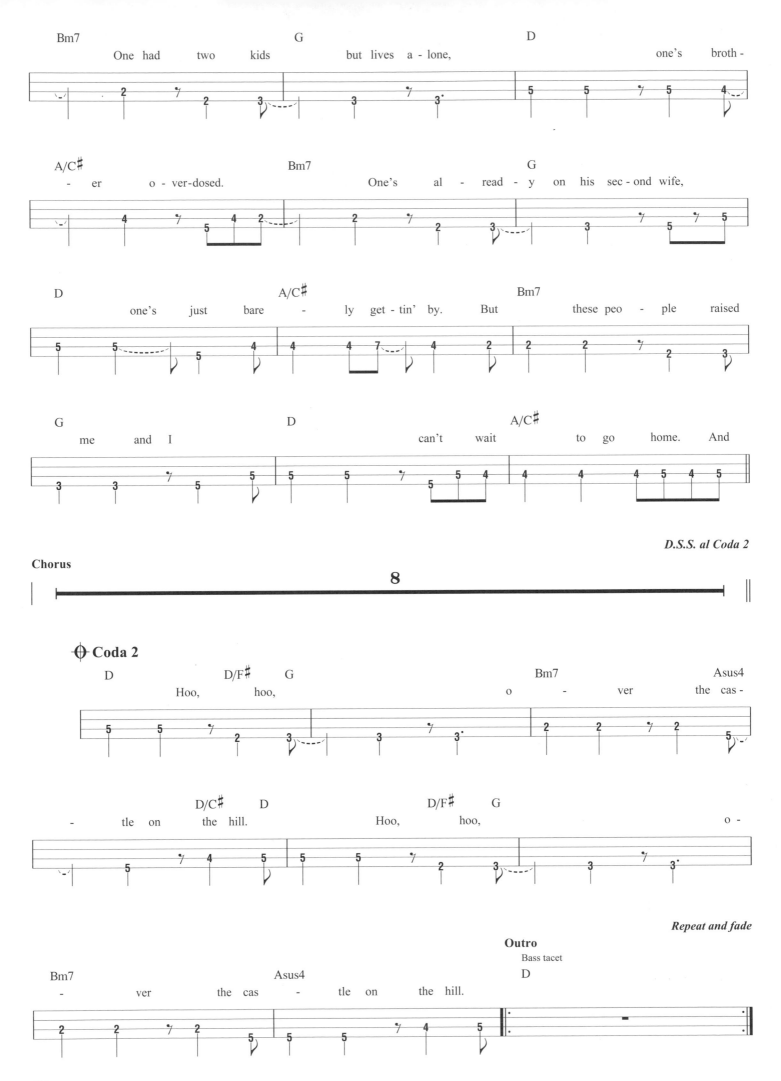

D.S.S. al Coda 2

Chorus

Repeat and fade

Cool Kids

Words and Music by Graham Sierota, Jamie Sierota, Noah Sierota,
Sydney Sierota, Jeffrey David Sierota and Jesiah Dzwonek

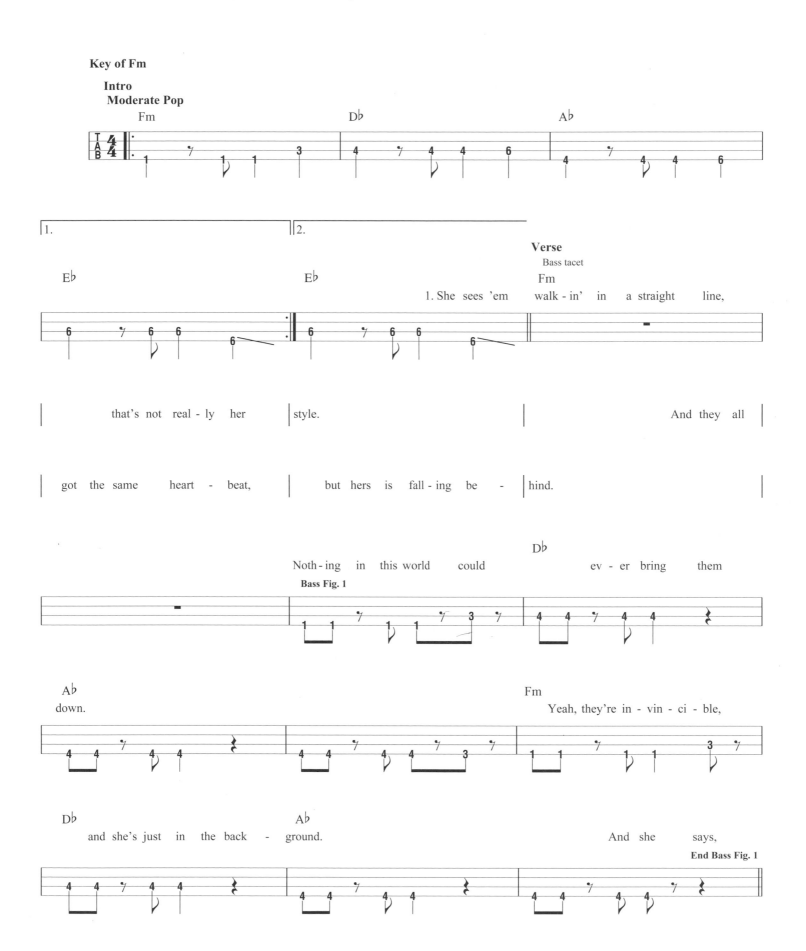

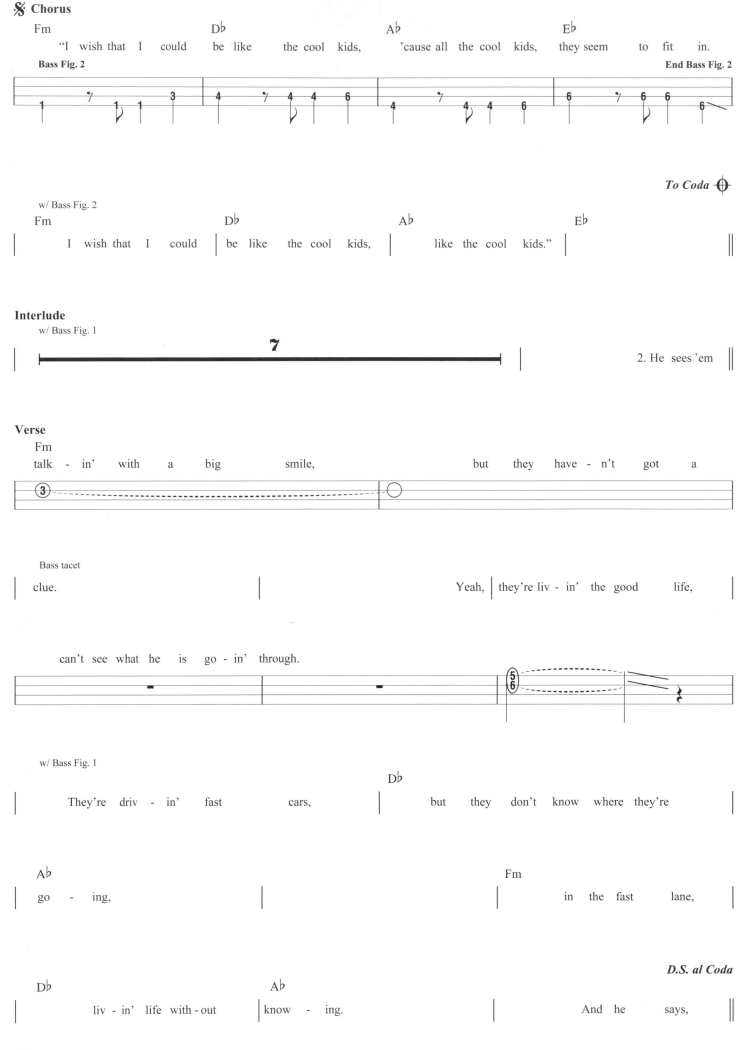

28

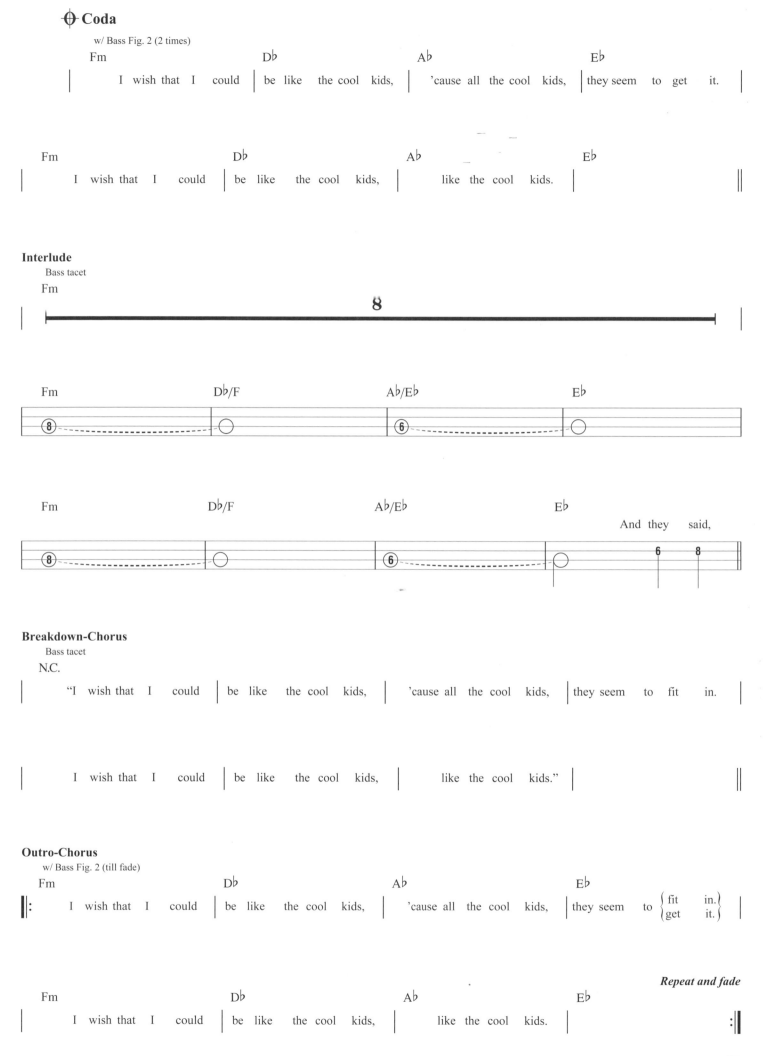

⊕ **Coda**

w/ Bass Fig. 2 (2 times)

Fm ... Db ... Ab ... Eb
| I wish that I could | be like the cool kids, | 'cause all the cool kids, | they seem to get it. |

Fm ... Db ... Ab ... Eb
| I wish that I could | be like the cool kids, | like the cool kids. |

Interlude

Bass tacet

Fm

8

Fm ... Db/F ... Ab/Eb ... Eb

Fm ... Db/F ... Ab/Eb ... Eb

And they said,

Breakdown-Chorus

Bass tacet

N.C.

| "I wish that I could | be like the cool kids, | 'cause all the cool kids, | they seem to fit in. |

| I wish that I could | be like the cool kids, | like the cool kids." |

Outro-Chorus

w/ Bass Fig. 2 (till fade)

Fm ... Db ... Ab ... Eb

| I wish that I could | be like the cool kids, | 'cause all the cool kids, | they seem to { fit in. } { get it. } |

Repeat and fade

Fm ... Db ... Ab ... Eb

| I wish that I could | be like the cool kids, | like the cool kids. |

Counting Stars

Words and Music by Ryan Tedder

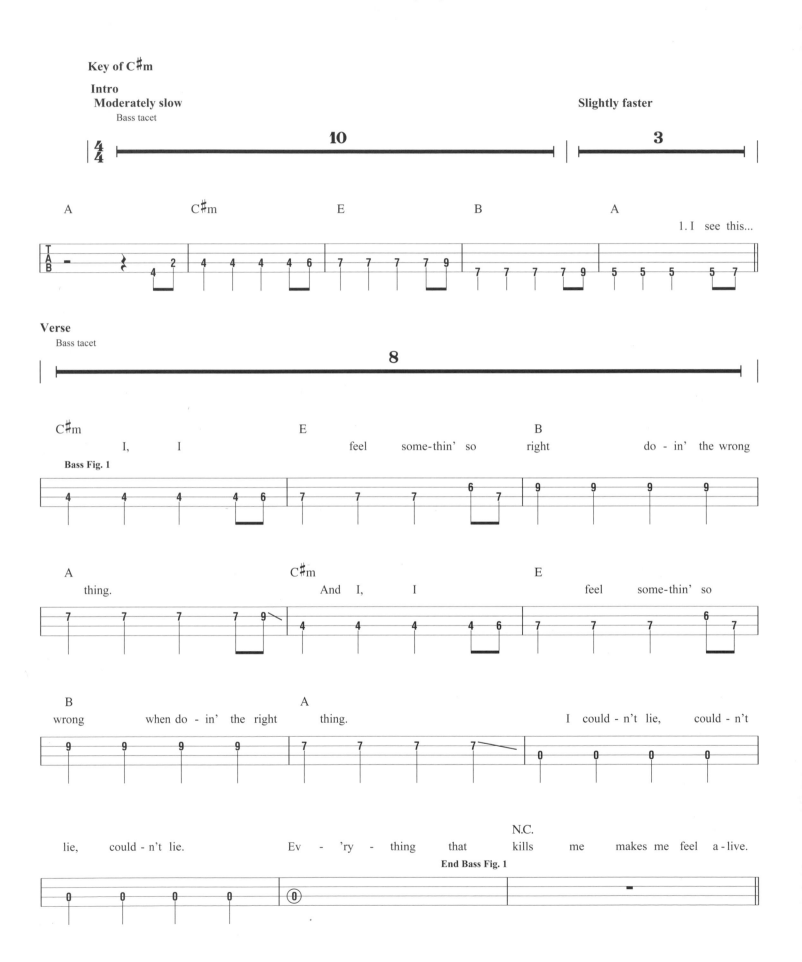

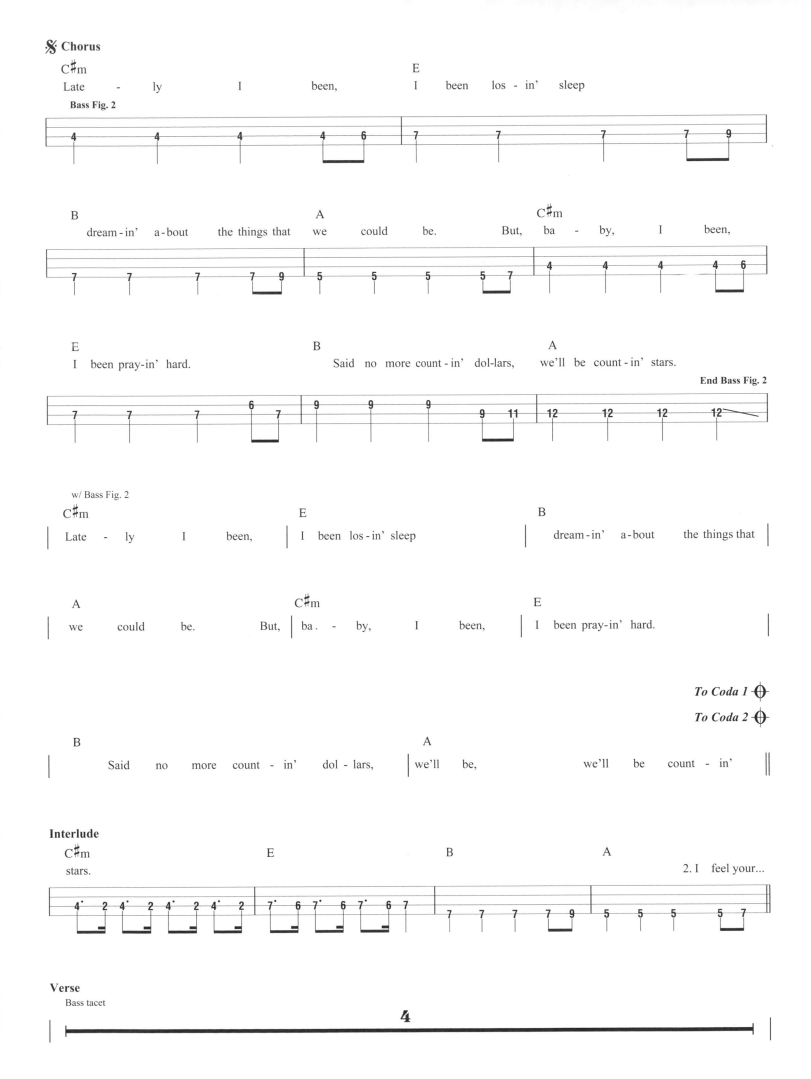

w/ Bass Fig. 1

C#m

Old, but I'm not that old.

E

Young, but I'm not that bold. And

B

I don't think the world is sold

A

on just do - in' what we're told.

C#m

And I, I

E

feel some - thin' so

B

wrong when do - in' the right

A

thing.

I could - n't lie, could - n't

D.S. al Coda 1

lie, could - n't lie.

N.C.

Ev - 'ry - thing that drowns me makes me wan - na fly.

⊕ Coda 1

Bridge

Bass tacet

| 2 | 8 |

D.S. al Coda 2

A tempo

A

Ev - 'ry - thing that kills me makes me feel a - live.

rit.

⊕ Coda 2

Outro

C#m

Take that mon - ey, watch it burn.

E

Sink in the riv - er the les - sons I've learned.

B

Take that mon - ey, watch it burn.

A

Sink in the riv - er the les - sons I've learned.

C#m

Take that mon - ey, watch it burn.

E

Sink in the riv - er the les - sons I've learned.

B

Take that mon - ey, watch it burn.

N.C.

Sink in the riv - er the les - sons I've learned.

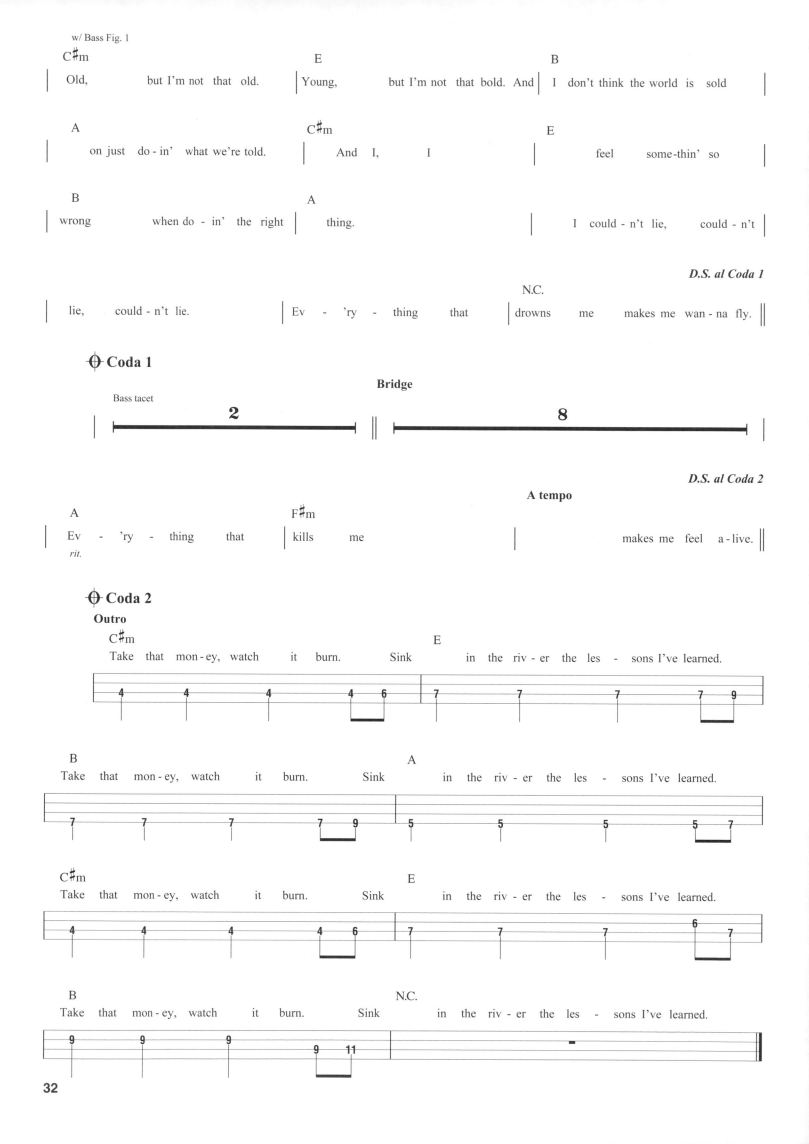

Happy

from DESPICABLE ME 2
Words and Music by Pharrell Williams

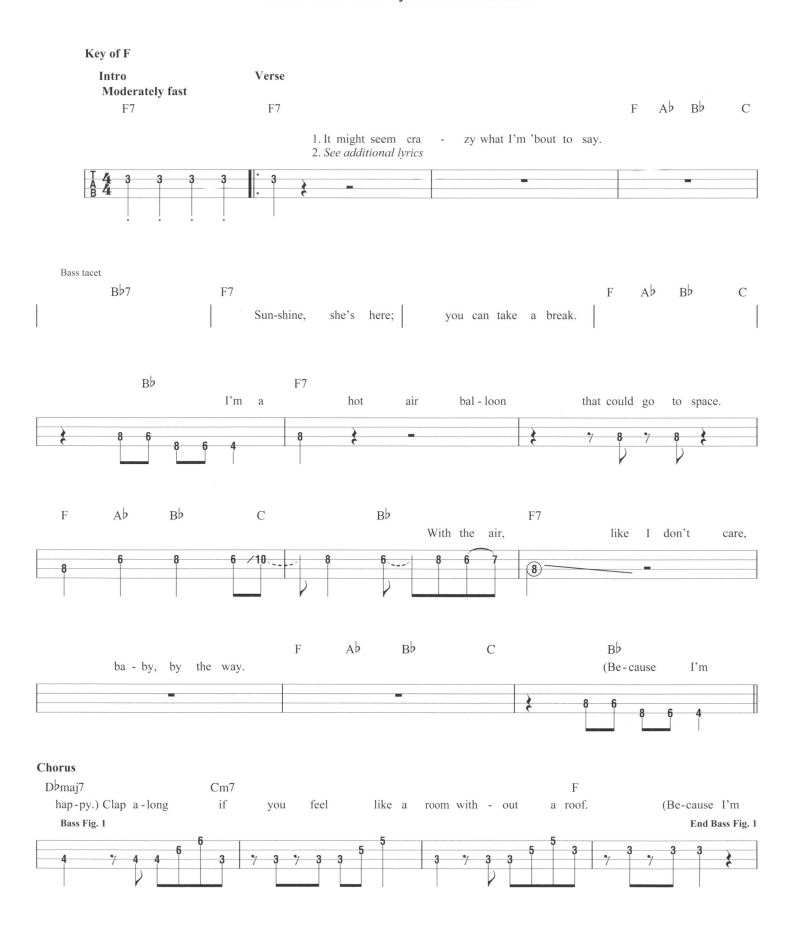

w/ Bass Fig. 1 (3 times)

D♭maj7		Cm7					F	
hap - py.) Clap a - long	if	you feel like	hap - pi - ness is the truth.				(Be-cause I'm	

D♭maj7		Cm7					F	
hap - py.) Clap a - long	if	you know what	hap - pi - ness is to you.				(Be-cause I'm	

D♭maj7		Cm7					F	
hap - py.) Clap a - long	if	you feel like	that's what you wan - na do.				:‖	

Interlude

N.C.(F5)

Bring me   down,   can't   noth - in'   bring me   down,   your love is too

Bass Fig. 2   End Bass Fig. 2

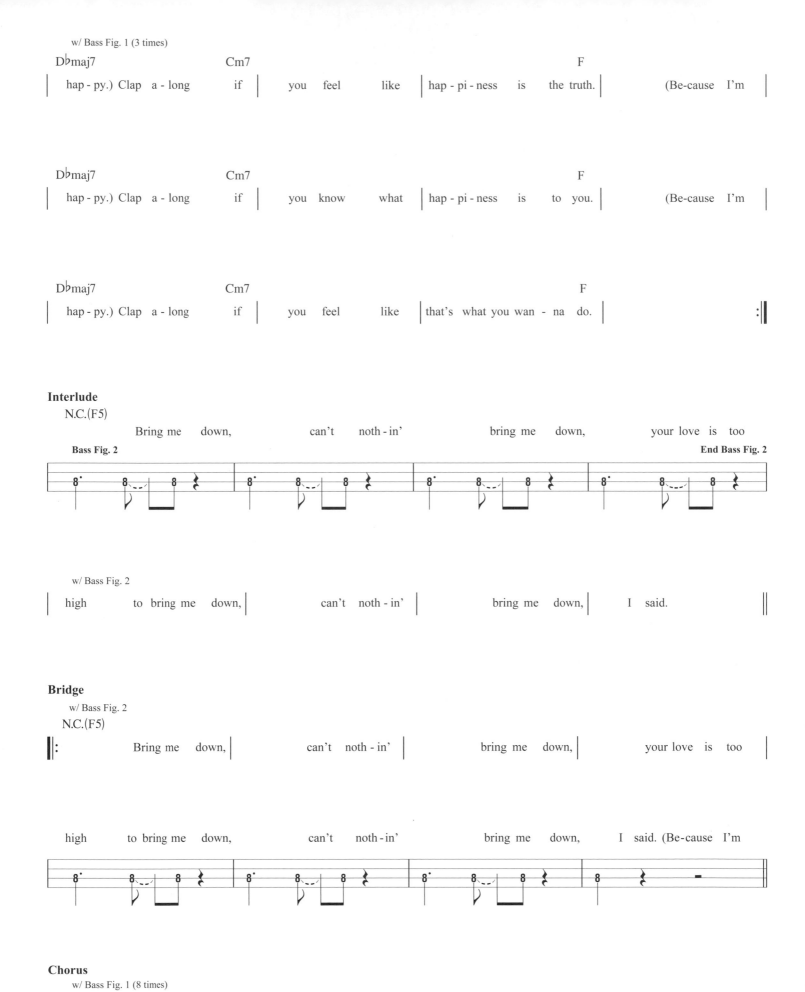

w/ Bass Fig. 2

high	to bring me down,		can't noth - in'	bring me down,	I said.	‖

Bridge

w/ Bass Fig. 2

N.C.(F5)

‖: Bring me   down,   can't   noth - in'   bring me   down,   your love is too

high   to bring me   down,   can't   noth - in'   bring me   down,   I said. (Be-cause I'm

Chorus

w/ Bass Fig. 1 (8 times)

D♭maj7		Cm7					F	
hap - py.) Clap a - long	if	you feel like a	room with - out a roof.				(Be-cause I'm	

Dbmaj7   **Cm7**   **F**

| hap - py.) Clap a - long | if | you feel like | hap - pi - ness is the truth. | (Be-cause I'm |

Dbmaj7   **Cm7**   **F**

| hap - py.) Clap a - long | if | you know what | hap - pi - ness is to you. | (Be-cause I'm |

Dbmaj7   **Cm7**   **F**

| hap - py.) Clap a - long | if | you feel like | that's what you wan - na do. | (Be-cause I'm |

Dbmaj7   **Cm7**   **F**

| hap - py.) Clap a - long | if | you feel like a | room with - out a roof. | (Be-cause I'm |

Dbmaj7   **Cm7**   **F**

| hap - py.) Clap a - long | if | you feel like | hap - pi - ness is the truth. | (Be-cause I'm |

Dbmaj7   **Cm7**   **F**

| hap - py.) Clap a - long | if | you know what | hap - pi - ness is to you. | (Be-cause I'm |

1.   2.

Dbmaj7   **Cm7**   **F**

| hap-py.) Clap a-long | if | you feel like | that's what you wan - na do. | :‖ Huh, come on. ‖

Additional Lyrics

2. Here come bad news, talkin' this and that.
   Well, gimme all you got and don't hold it back.
   Well, I should prob'ly warn you, I'll be just fine.
   No offense to you, don't waste your time.

Home

Words and Music by Greg Holden and Drew Pearson

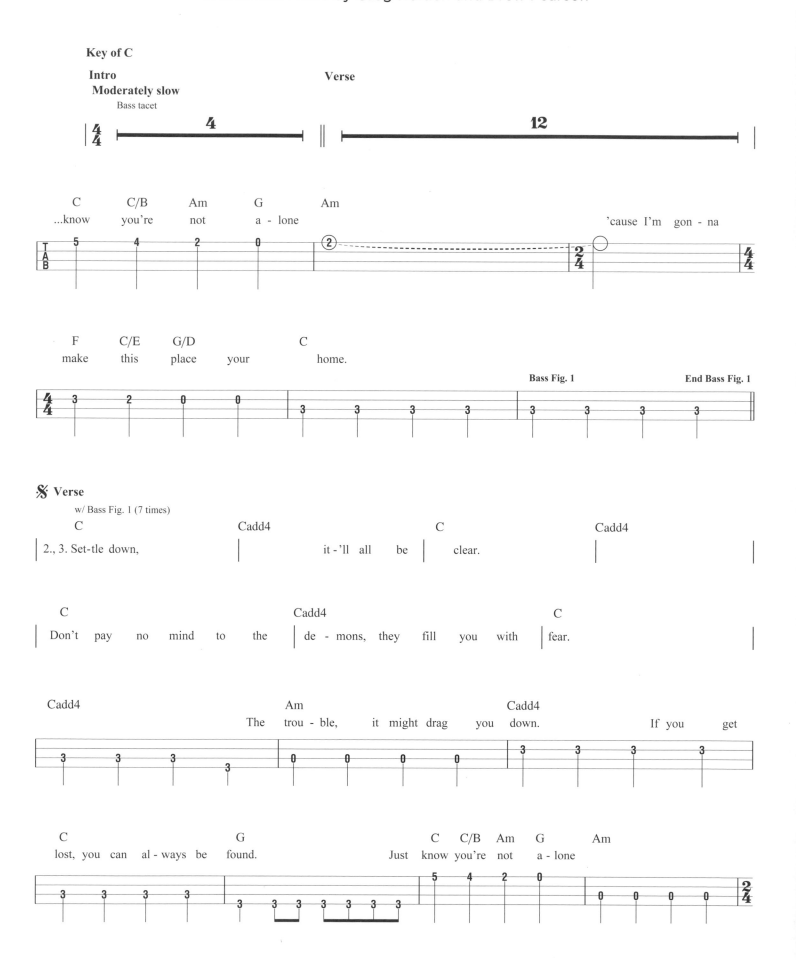

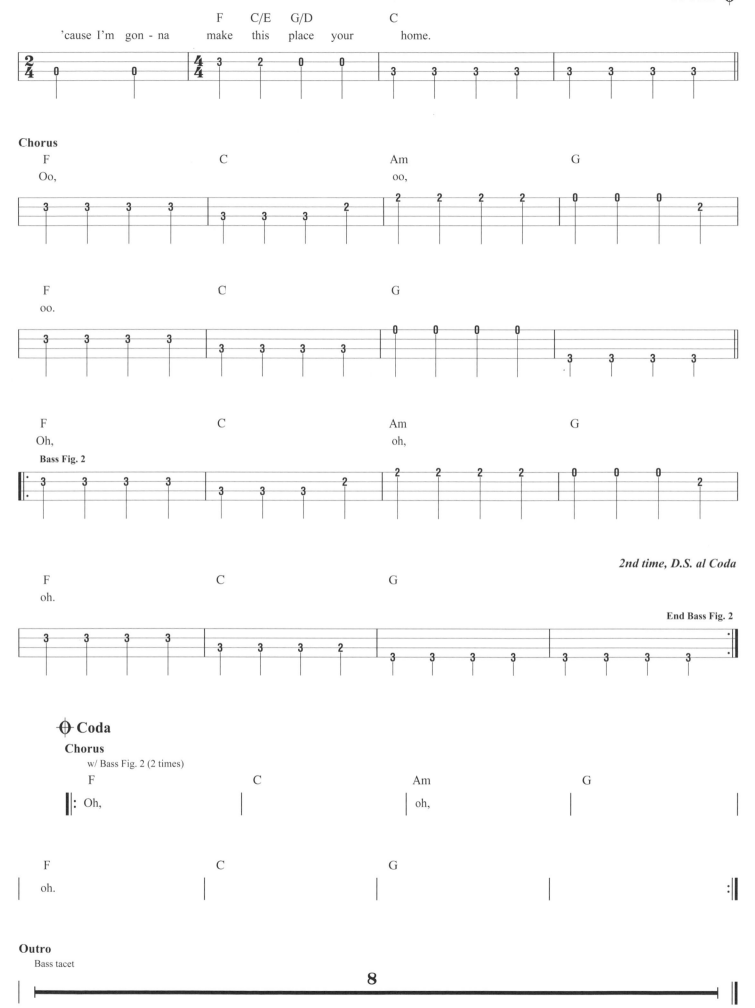

Just the Way You Are

Words and Music by Bruno Mars, Ari Levine, Philip Lawrence, Khari Cain and Khalil Walton

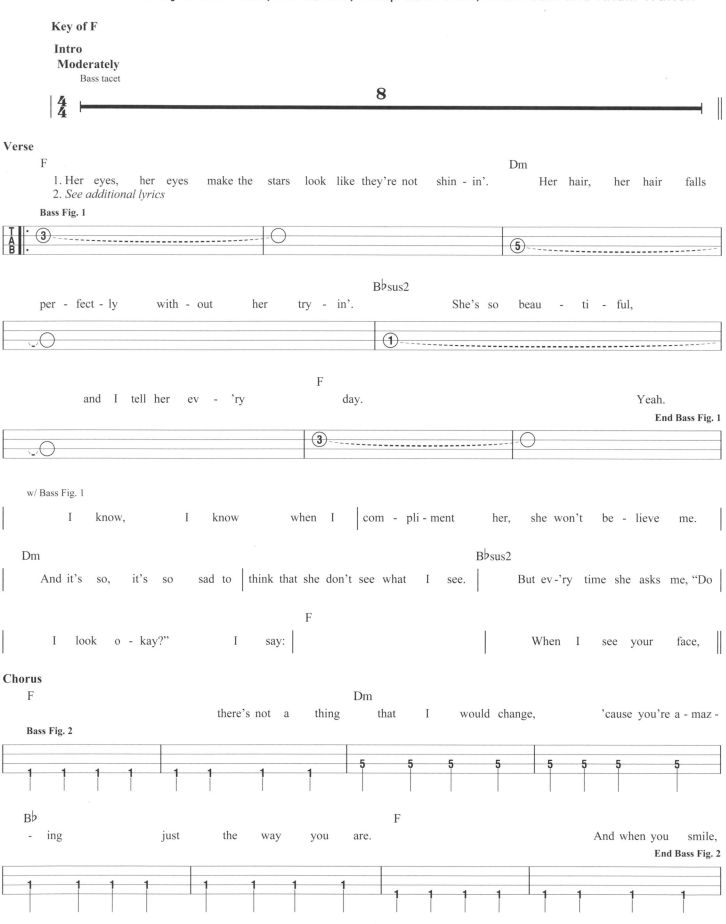

Key of F

Intro
Moderately
Bass tacet

Verse

F
1. Her eyes, her eyes make the stars look like they're not shin - in'. Dm Her hair, her hair falls
2. *See additional lyrics*

Bass Fig. 1

per - fect - ly with - out her try - in'. B♭sus2 She's so beau - ti - ful,

and I tell her ev - 'ry F day. Yeah.

End Bass Fig. 1

w/ Bass Fig. 1

I know, I know when I com - pli - ment her, she won't be - lieve me.

Dm And it's so, it's so sad to think that she don't see what I see. B♭sus2 But ev -'ry time she asks me, "Do

I look o - kay?" I say: F When I see your face,

Chorus

F there's not a thing that I would change, Dm 'cause you're a - maz -

Bass Fig. 2

- ing just the way you are. B♭ And when you smile, F

End Bass Fig. 2

Dm

the whole world stops   and stares for a while,   'cause, girl, you're a - maz -

|1. |2.

Bb   F

- ing   just   the way you are.   Yeah.   :|| The way you are,

w/ Bass Fig. 2

Dm

the way you are.   Girl, you're a - maz -

Bb   F

- ing   just   the way you are.   When I see your face,

Outro-Chorus

Bass tacet

F   Dm

there's not a thing that I would change,   'cause you're a - maz -

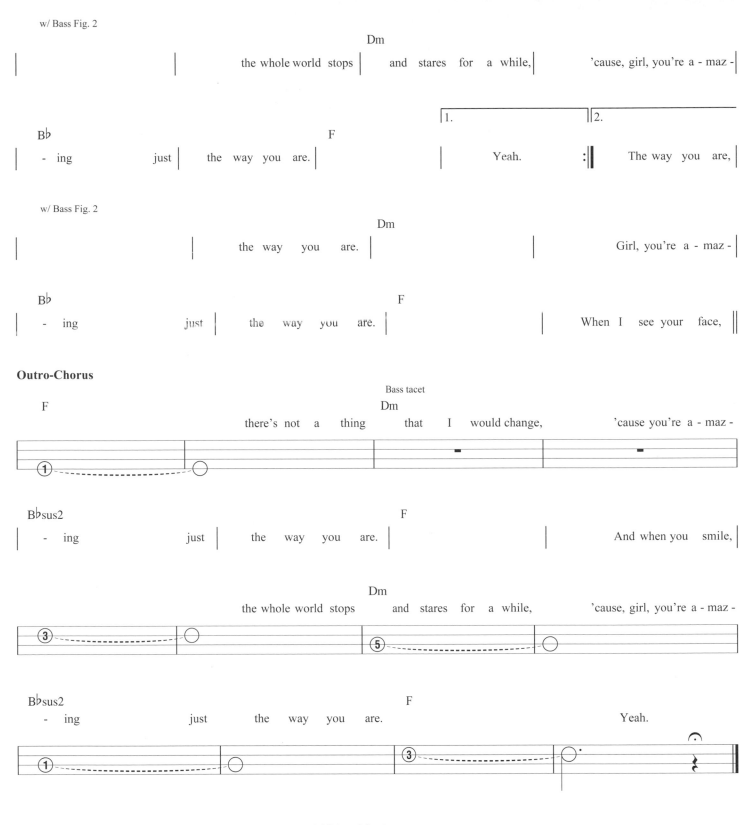

Bbsus2   F

- ing   just   the way you are.   And when you smile,

Dm

the whole world stops   and stares for a while,   'cause, girl, you're a - maz -

Bbsus2   F

- ing   just   the way you are.   Yeah.

Additional Lyrics

2. Her lips, her lips,
   I could kiss them all day if she'd let me.
   Her laugh, her laugh,
   She hates but I think it's so sexy.
   She's so beautiful,
   And I tell her ev'ry day.
   Oh, you know, you know,
   You know I'd never ask you to change.
   If perfect's what you're searchin' for
   Then just stay the same.
   So don't even bother askin' if you look okay.
   You know I'll say:

Roar

Words and Music by Katy Perry, Max Martin, Dr. Luke, Bonnie McKee and Henry Walter

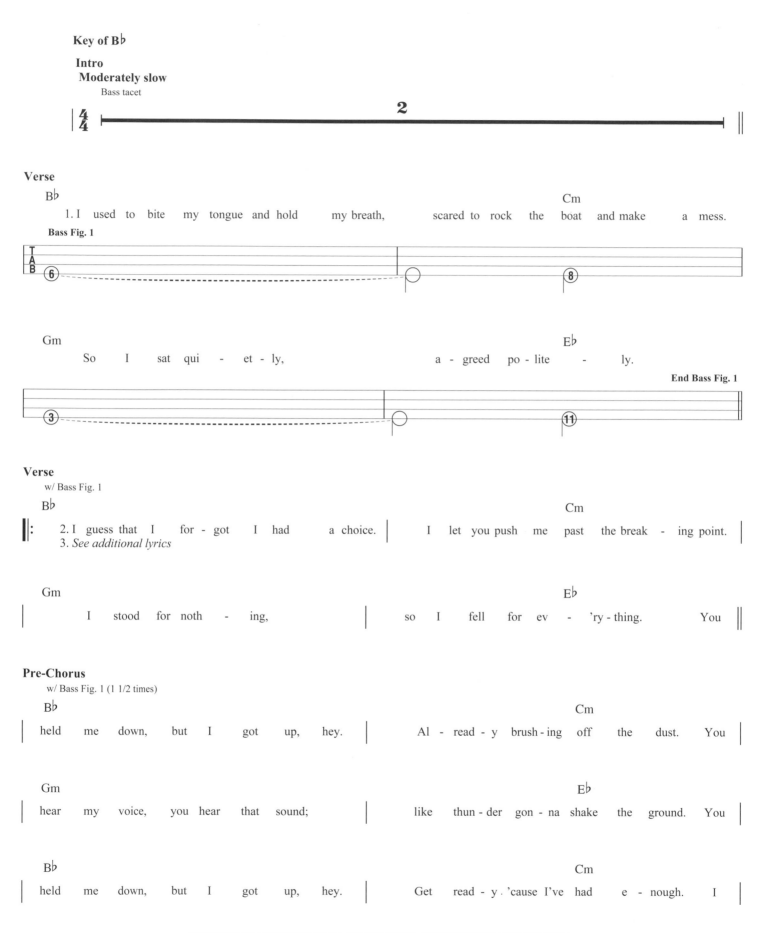

Key of B♭

Intro
Moderately slow
Bass tacet

Verse

B♭
1. I used to bite my tongue and hold my breath,   scared to rock the boat and make a mess. *(Cm)*

Bass Fig. 1

Gm
So I sat qui - et - ly,   a - greed po - lite - ly. *(E♭)*

End Bass Fig. 1

Verse
w/ Bass Fig. 1

B♭
2. I guess that I for - got I had a choice.   I let you push me past the break - ing point. *(Cm)*
3. *See additional lyrics*

Gm
I stood for noth - ing,   so I fell for ev - 'ry - thing. You *(E♭)*

Pre-Chorus
w/ Bass Fig. 1 (1 1/2 times)

B♭
held me down, but I got up, hey.   Al - read - y brush - ing off the dust. You *(Cm)*

Gm
hear my voice, you hear that sound;   like thun - der gon - na shake the ground. You *(E♭)*

B♭
held me down, but I got up, hey.   Get read - y 'cause I've had e - nough. I *(Cm)*

Chorus

Gm ... see it all, I see it now. Eb N.C. I got the eye of the ti - Bb ger, a fight - er, danc -

Bass Fig. 2

Cm ing through the fire. Gm 'Cause I am a cham - pion and you're gon - na hear me Eb roar.

End Bass Fig. 2

w/ Bass Fig. 2 (2 times)

Bb Loud - er, loud - er than a li - on 'cause I Cm am a cham - pion and Gm

Eb you're gon - na hear me Bb roar. Oh, Cm

1.
Bass tacet

Gm oh. You're gon - na hear me Eb roar. Bb N.C.

2.
To Coda

Bb Oh, Cm oh. Gm You're gon - na hear me Eb roar.

Bridge

Bb Cm Gm F Roar, oh,

grad. cresc.

D.S. al Coda
(take 2nd ending)

Coda

roar, oh, roar. N.C. I got the eye of the ti - Bb

Additional Lyrics

3. Now I'm floatin' like a butterfly.
   Stingin' like a bee, I earned my stripes.
   I went from zero to my own hero.

Rude

Words and Music by Nasri Atweh, Mark Pellizzer, Alex Tanas, Ben Spivak and Adam Messinger

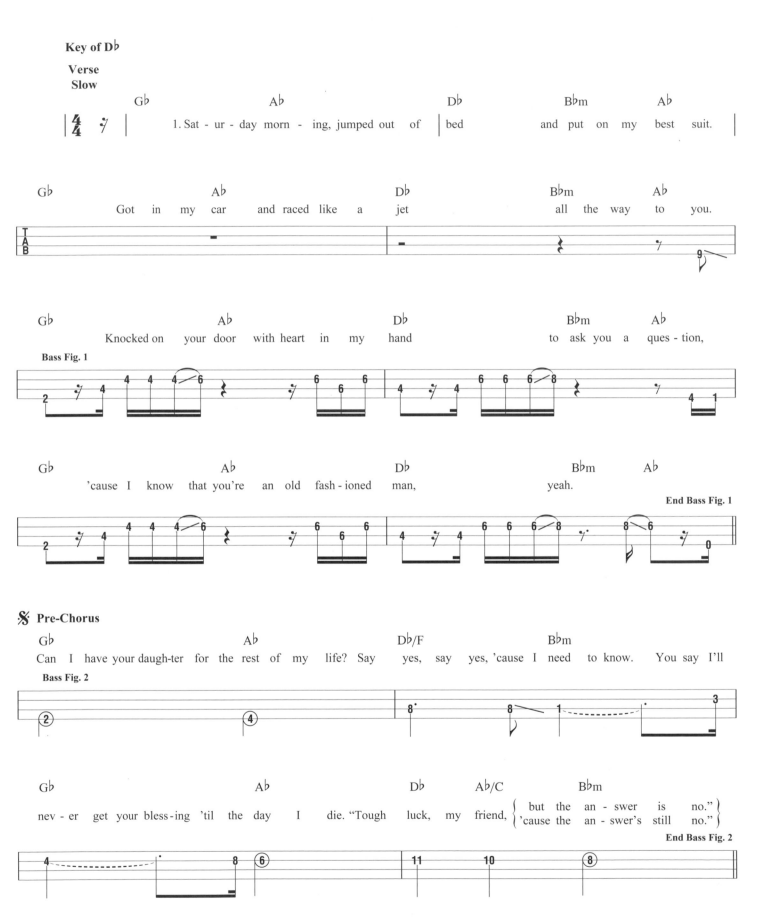

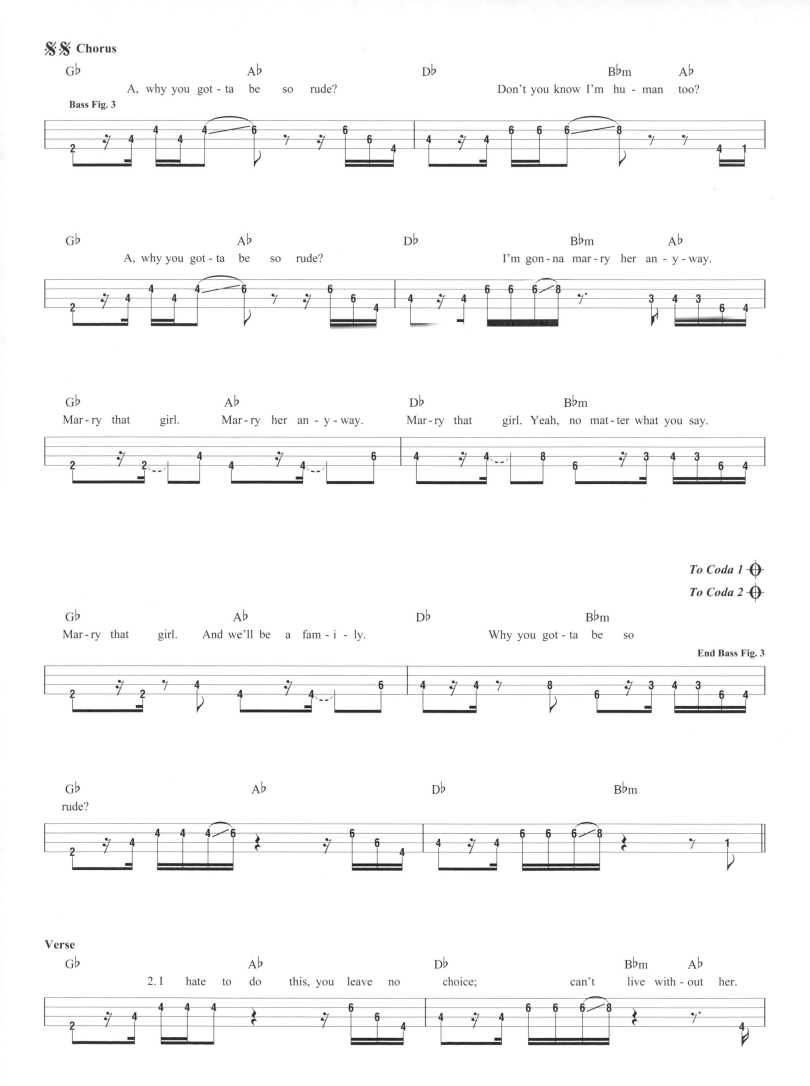

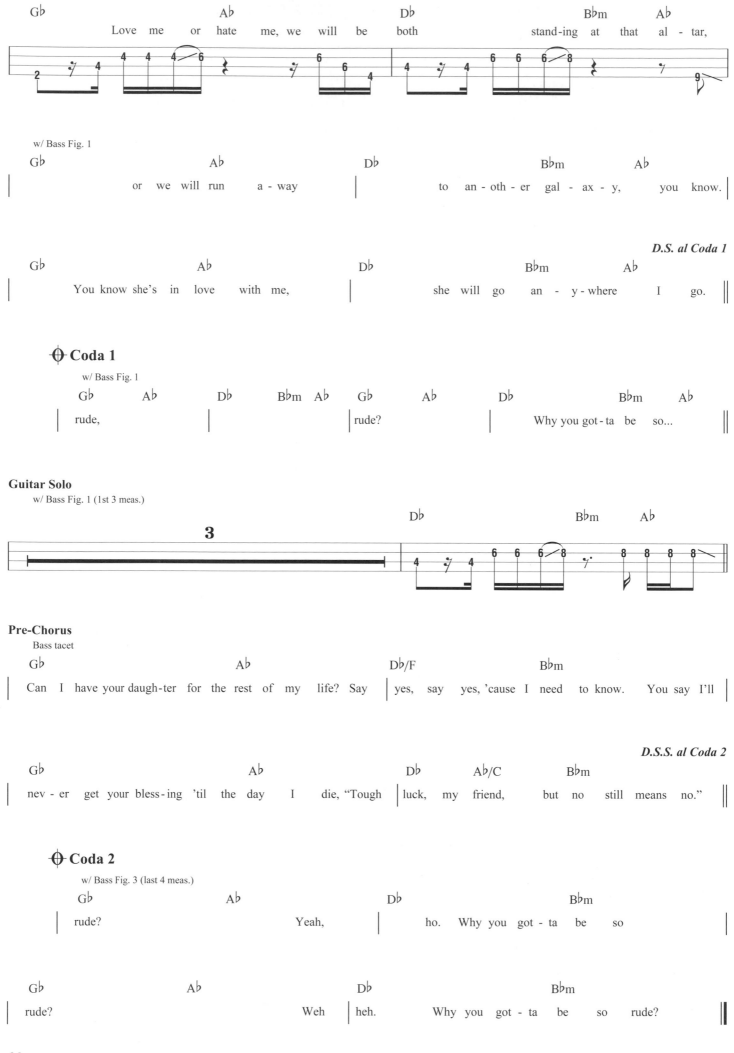

Shut Up and Dance

Words and Music by Ryan McMahon, Ben Berger, Sean Waugaman,
Eli Maiman, Nicholas Petricca and Kevin Ray

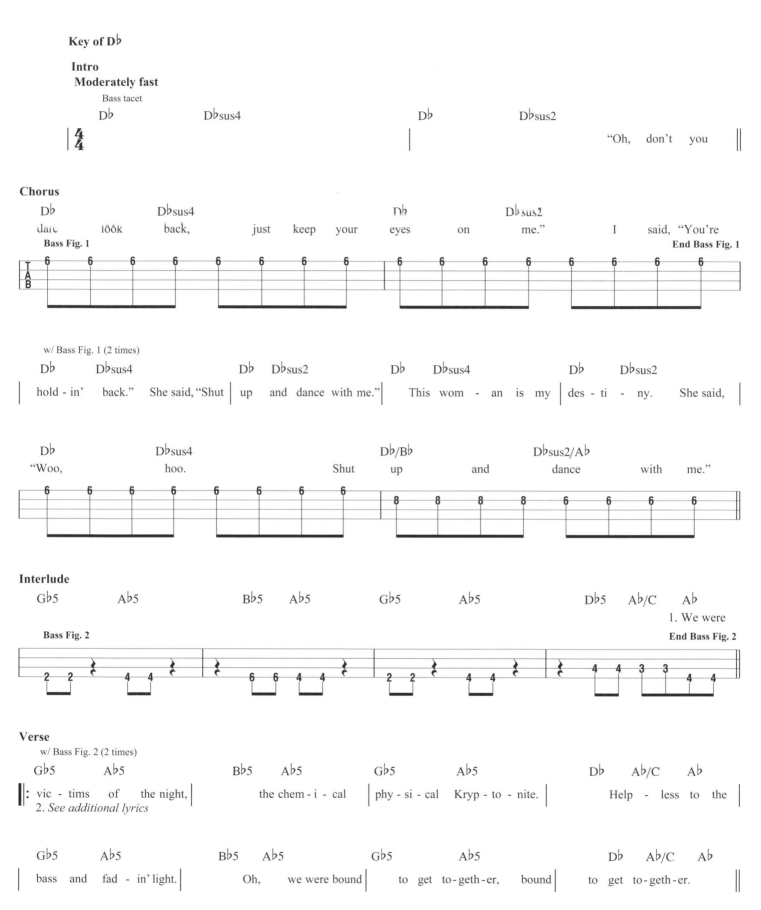

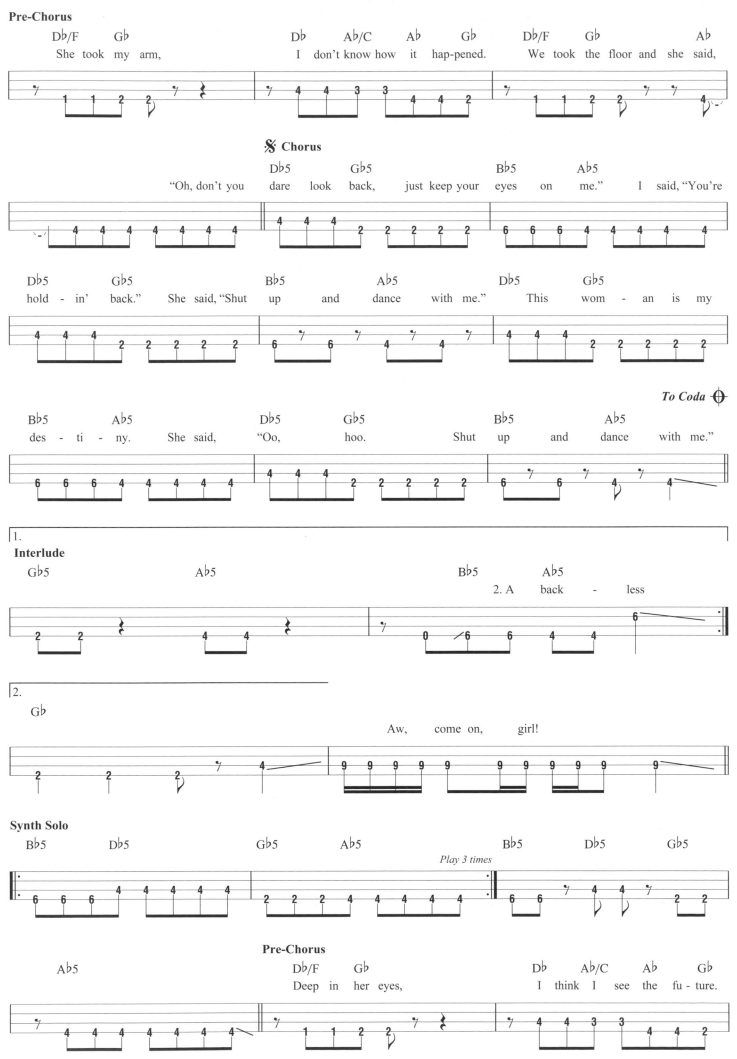

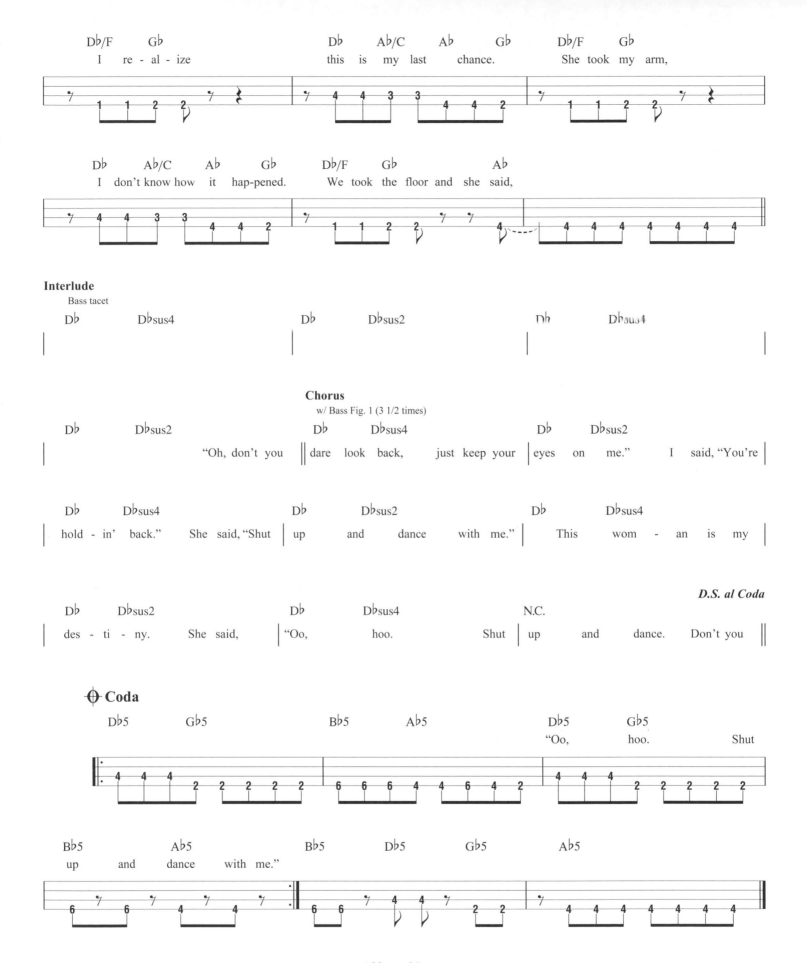

Additional Lyrics

2. A backless dress and some beat-up sneaks,
My discotech Juliette teenage dream.
I felt it in my chest as she looked at me.
I knew we were bound to be together,
Bound to be together.

Seven Nation Army

Words and Music by Jack White

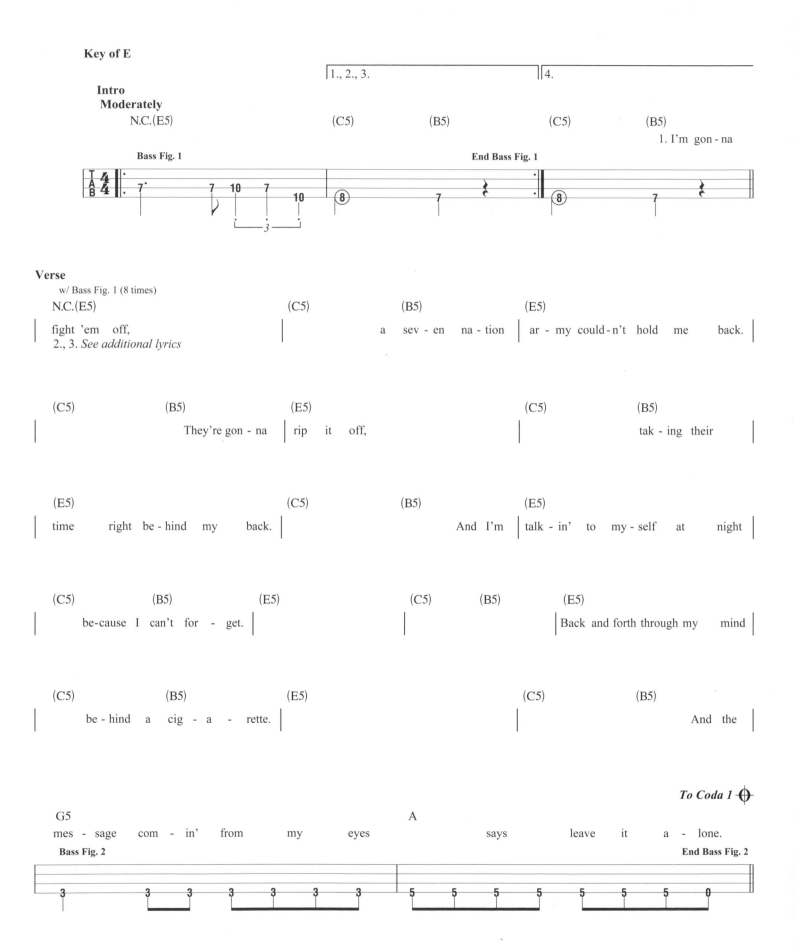

Interlude

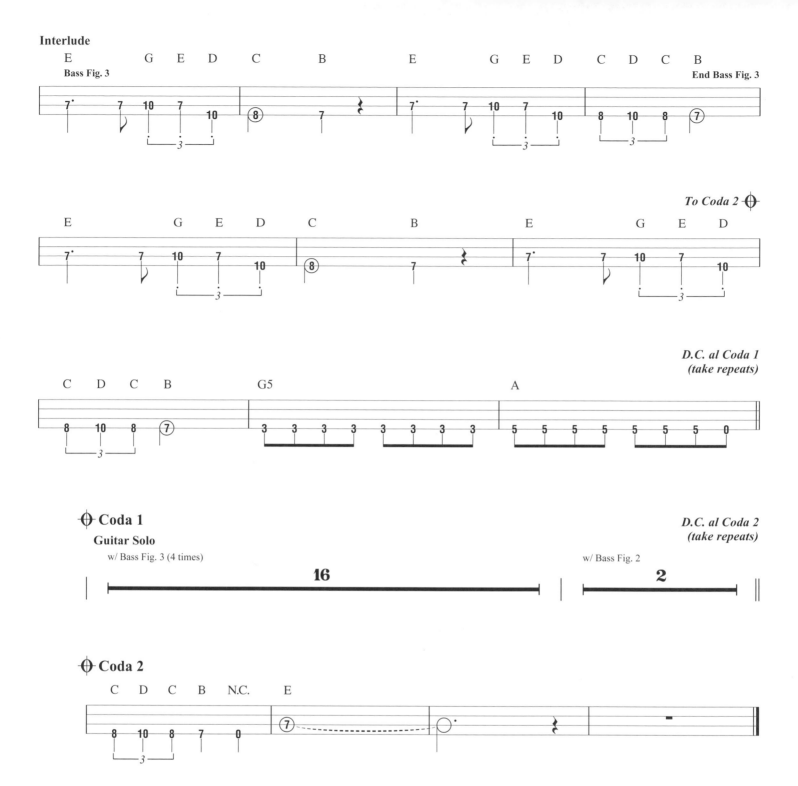

Additional Lyrics

2. Don't wanna hear about it, ev'ry single one's got a story to tell.
   Ev'ryone knows about it, from the Queen of England to the hounds of hell.
   And if I catch it coming back my way, I'm gonna serve it to you.
   And that ain't what you want to hear, but that's what I'll do.
   And the feeling coming from my bones says find a home.

3. I'm goin' to Wichita, far from this opera forevermore.
   I'm gonna work the straw, make the sweat drip out of every pore.
   And I'm bleeding, and I'm bleeding, and I'm bleeding right before the Lord.
   All the words are gonna bleed from me and I will think no more.
   And the stains coming from my blood tell me go back home.

Stereo Hearts

Words and Music by Brandon Lowry, Dan Omelio, Adam Levine, Ammar Malik, Benjamin Levin,
Travis McCoy, Disashi Lumumba-Kasongo, Matthew McGinley and Eric Roberts

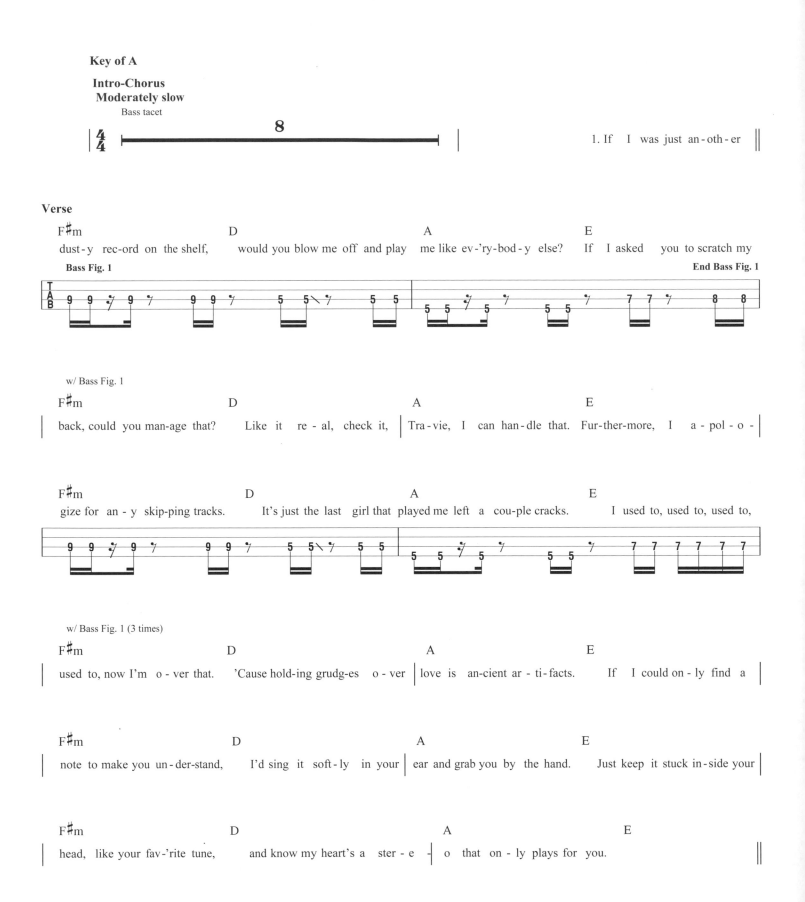

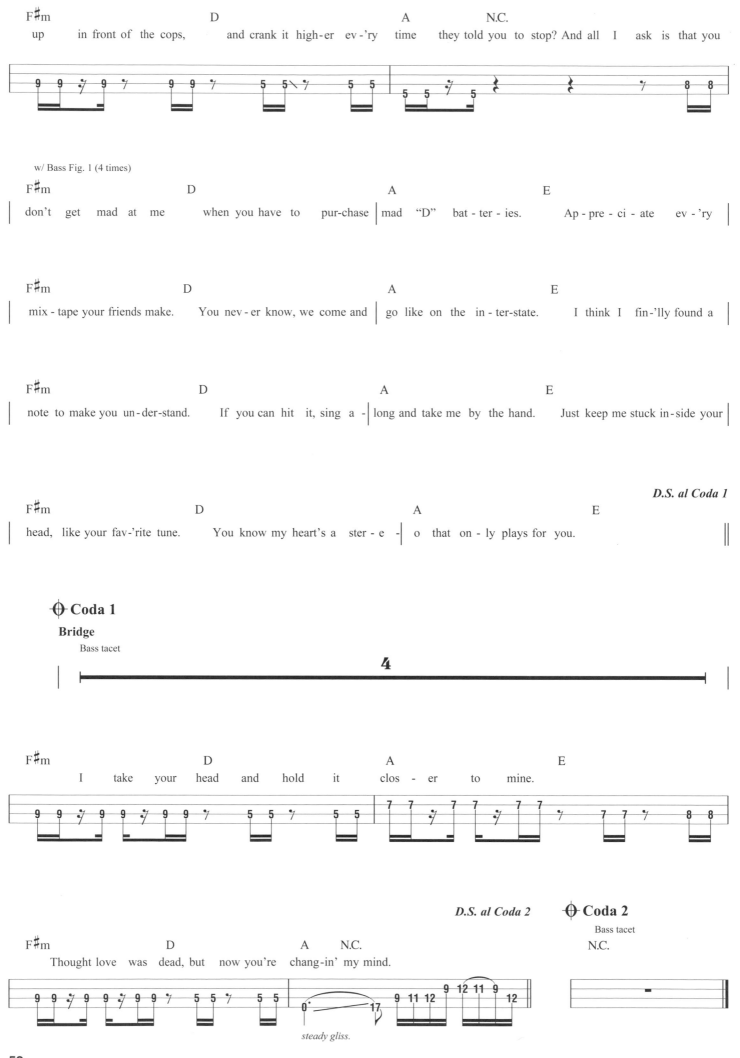

Superheroes

Words and Music by Danny O'Donoghue, Mark Sheehan and James Barry

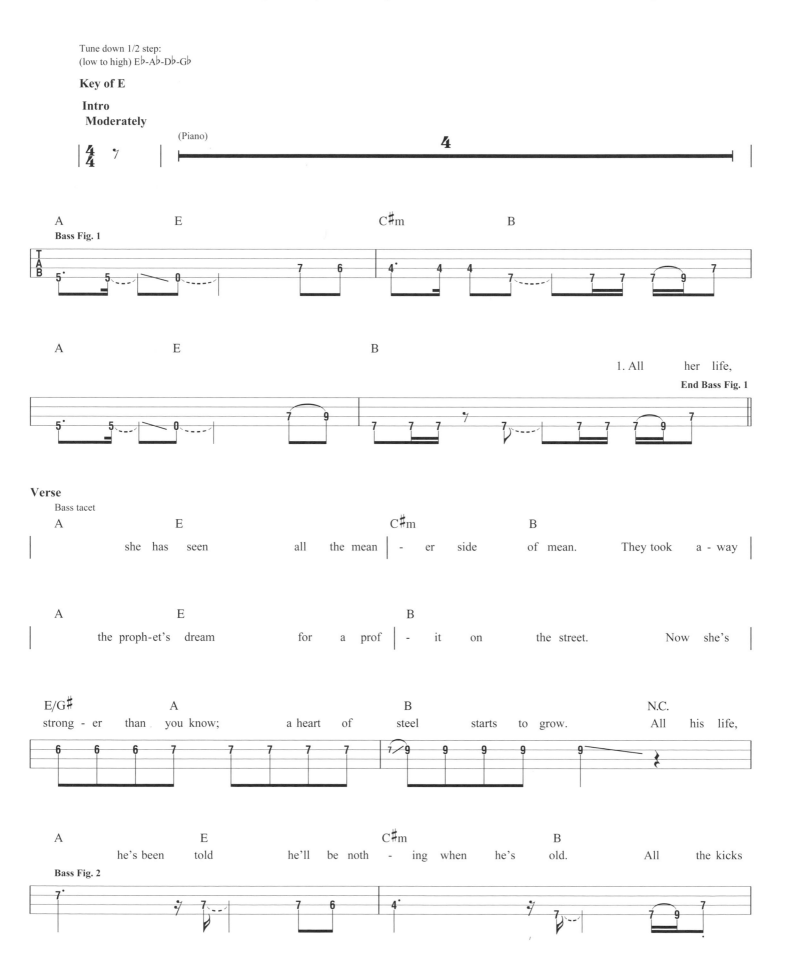

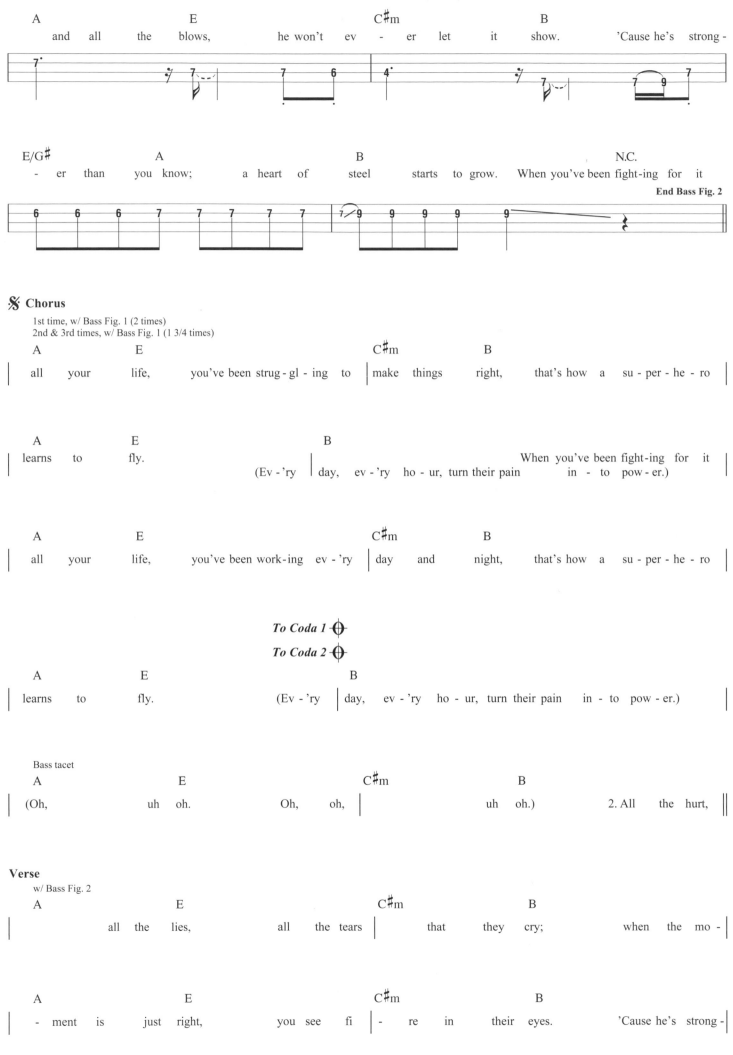

E/G#   A   B   N.C.

-er than   you know;   a heart of | steel   starts   to grow.   When you've been fight-ing for   it

⊕ Coda 1

Interlude
w/ Bass Fig. 1 (2 times)

B

day, ev -'ry ho - ur, turn their pain   in - to pow - er.)

7 7 7 𝄾   7 7 7 7 7 𝄾

8

Bridge
Bass tacet

4

F#m   E/A

...li - ons in her heart,   a fire   in her soul. He's got a

4·   4 𝄾   7   7

E   B   E/G#   A

beast in his bel - ly that's so hard to con - trol.   'Cause they've tak - en too much hits, take 'em blow   by blow.   Now,

2·   2   2   6   6   6   7   7   7   7

D.S. al Coda 2

B   N.C.

light a match, stand back, watch 'em ex-plode,   ex-plode,   ex-plode,   ex-plode, ex-plode.   When you've been fight-ing for   it

7·9 9 9 9 9 9 9 9 9 9 9 9 9 9 𝄾

⊕ Coda 2

Outro
w/ Bass Fig. 1 (2 times)

B

day, ev -'ry ho - ur, turn their pain   in - to pow - er.)

7 7 7 𝄾   7 7 7 7 7 𝄾

8

Bass tacet

4

𝄐

Wake Me Up

Words and Music by Aloe Blacc, Tim Bergling and Michael Einziger

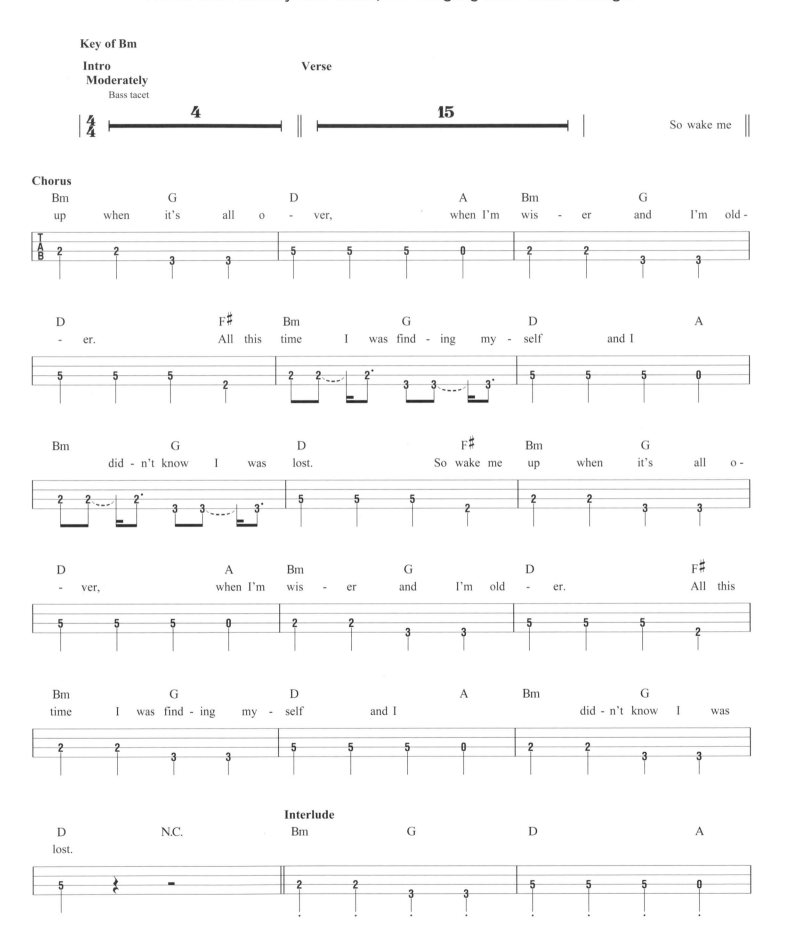

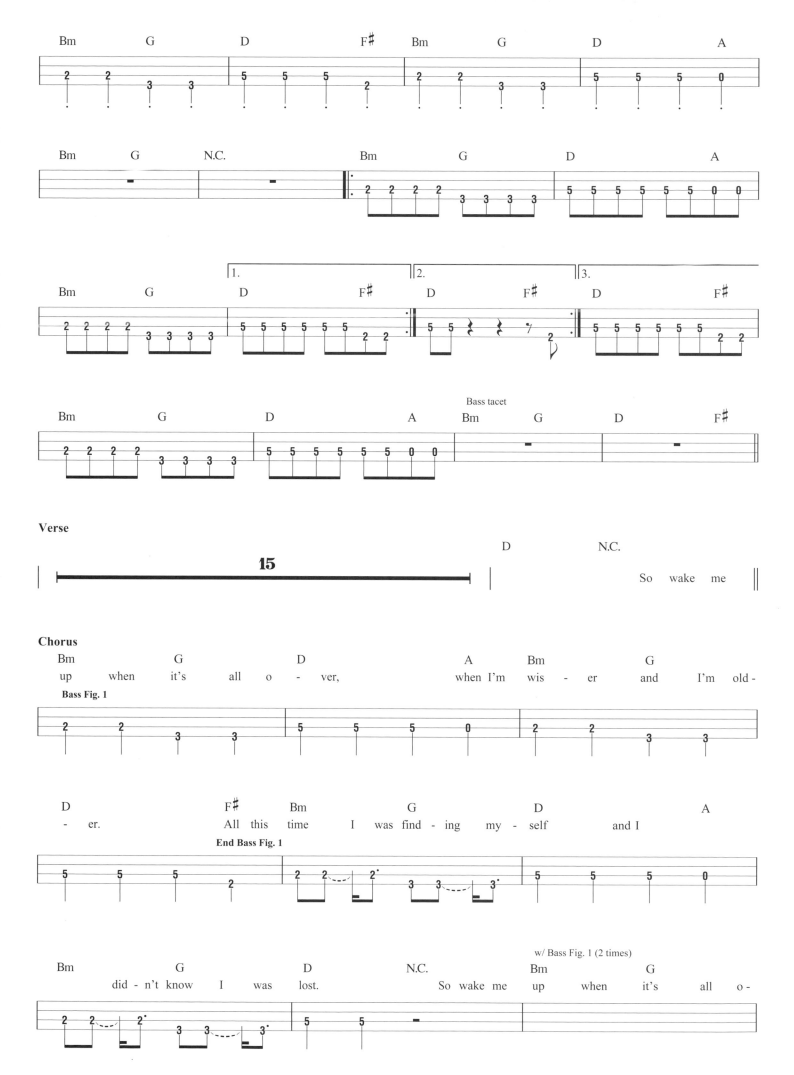

Verse

Chorus

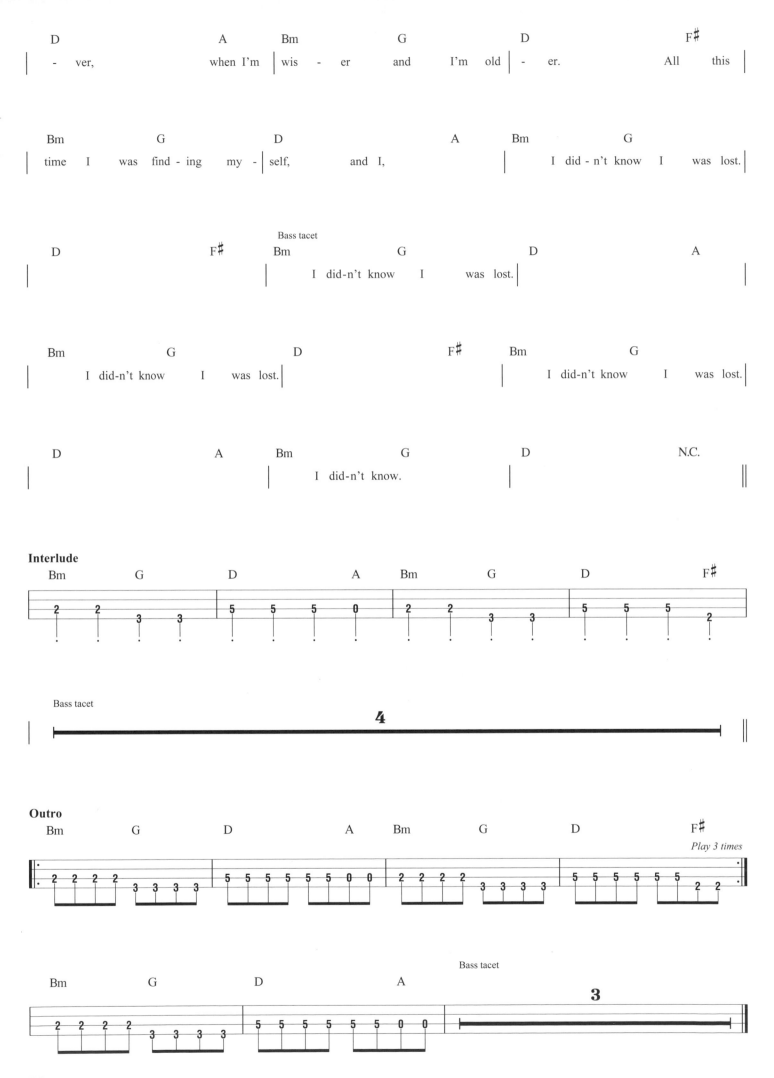

What Makes You Beautiful

Words and Music by Savan Kotecha, Rami Yacoub and Carl Falk

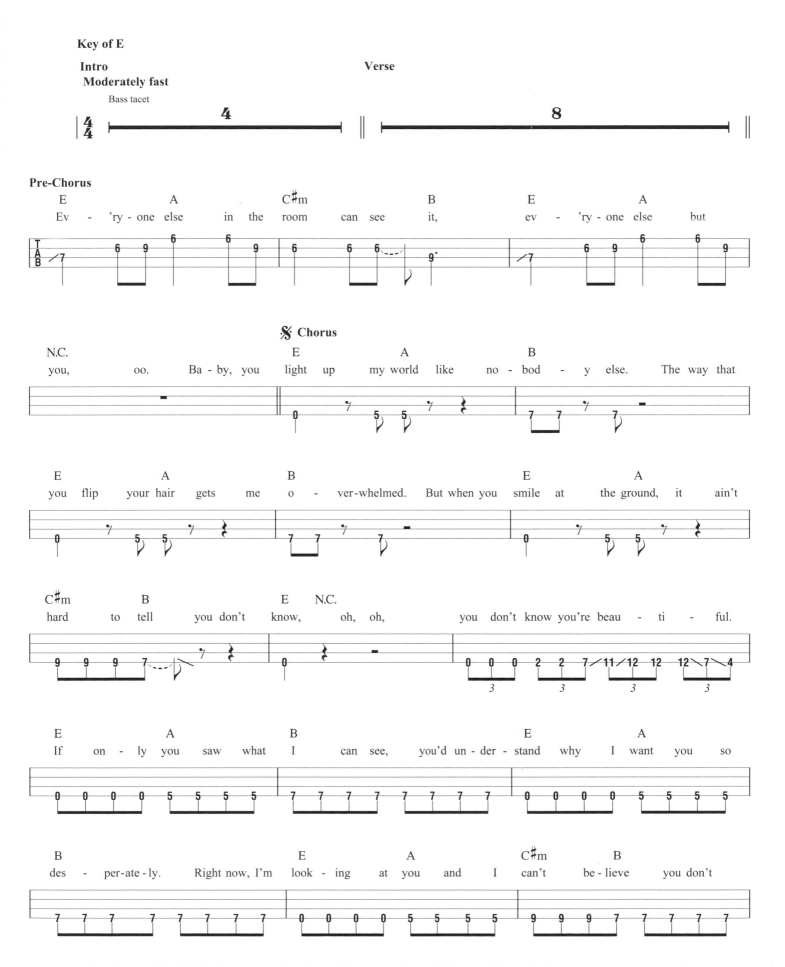

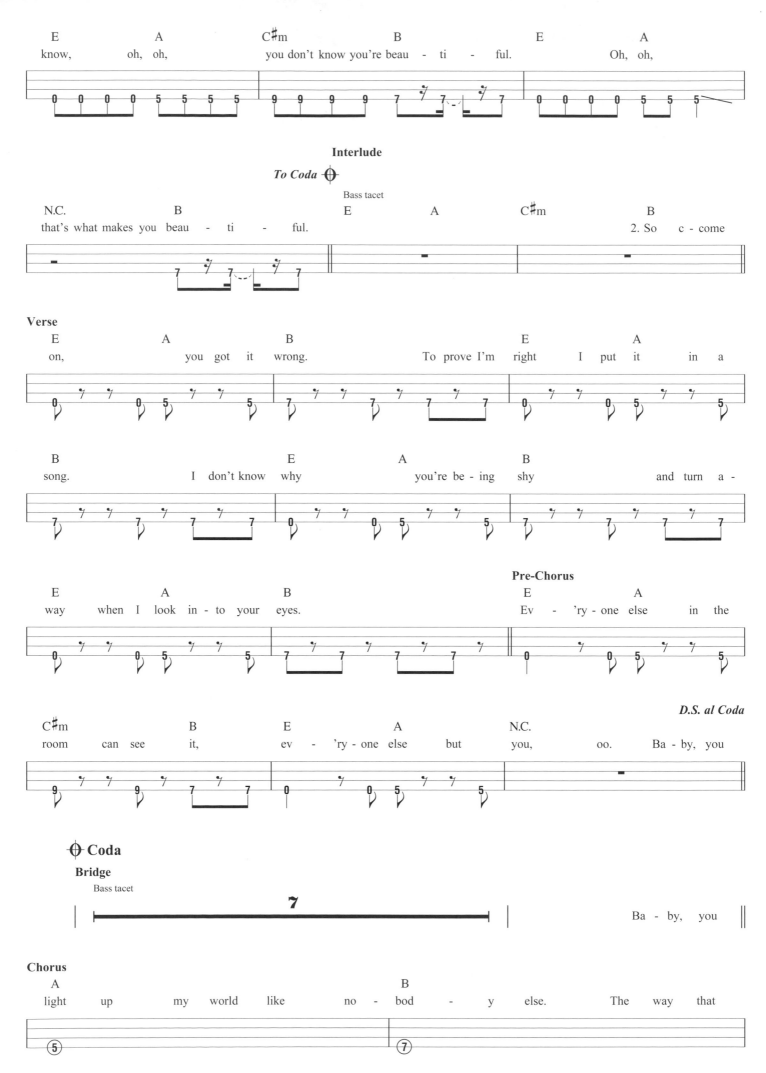

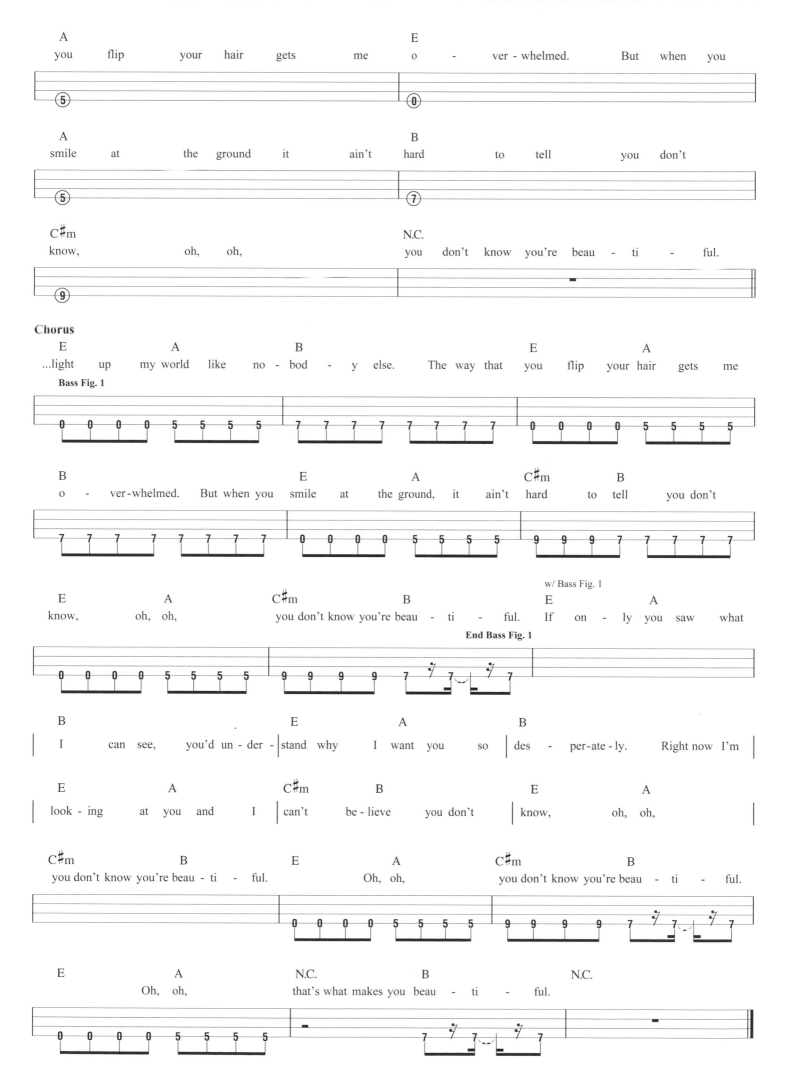

HAL LEONARD BASS METHOD

METHOD BOOKS

by Ed Friedland

BOOK 1

Book 1 teaches: tuning; playing position; musical symbols; notes within the first five frets; common bass lines, patterns and rhythms; rhythms through eighth notes; playing tips and techniques; more than 100 great songs, riffs and examples; and more! The audio includes 44 full-band tracks for demonstration or play-along.
00695067 Book Only $7.99
00695068 Book/Online Audio $12.99

BOOK 2

Book 2 continues where Book 1 left off and teaches: the box shape; moveable boxes; notes in fifth position; major and minor scales; the classic blues line; the shuffle rhythm; tablature; and more!
00695069 Book Only $7.99
00695070 Book/Online Audio $12.99

BOOK 3

With the third book, progressing students will learn more great songs, riffs and examples; sixteenth notes; playing off chord symbols; slap and pop techniques; hammer-ons and pull-offs; playing different styles and grooves; and more.
00695071 Book Only $7.99
00695072 Book/Online Audio $12.99

COMPOSITE

This money-saving edition contains Books 1, 2 and 3.
00695073 Book Only $17.99
00695074 Book/Online Audio $24.99

DVD

Play your favorite songs in no time with this DVD! Covers: tuning, notes in first through third position, rhythms through eighth notes, fingerstyle and pick playing, 4/4 and 3/4 time, and more! Includes 6 full songs and on-screen music notation. 68 minutes.
00695849 DVD $19.95

BASS FOR KIDS

by Chad Johnson

Bass for Kids is a fun, easy course that teaches children to play bass guitar faster than ever before. Popular songs such as "Crazy Train," "Every Breath You Take," "A Hard Day's Night" and "Wild Thing" keep kids motivated, and the clean, simple page layouts ensure their attention remains focused on one concept at a time.
00696449 Book/Online Audio $12.99

REFERENCE BOOKS

BASS SCALE FINDER

by Chad Johnson

Learn to use the entire fretboard with the *Bass Scale Finder*. This book contains over 1,300 scale diagrams for the most important 17 scale types.
00695781 6" x 9" Edition $7.99
00695778 9" x 12" Edition $7.99

BASS ARPEGGIO FINDER

by Chad Johnson

This extensive reference guide lays out over 1,300 arpeggio shapes. 28 different qualities are covered for each key, and each quality is presented in four different shapes.
00695817 6" x 9" Edition $7.99
00695816 9" x 12" Edition $7.99

MUSIC THEORY FOR BASSISTS

by Sean Malone

Acclaimed bassist and composer Sean Malone will explain the written language of music, using easy-to-understand terms and concepts, diagrams, and much more. The audio provides 96 tracks of examples, demonstrations, and play-alongs.
00695756 Book/Online Audio $17.99

STYLE BOOKS

BASS LICKS

by Ed Friedland

This comprehensive supplement to any bass method will help students learn over 200 great bass licks, lines and grooves in many rhythmic styles. *Bass Licks* illustrates how simple melodic patterns can become the springboard for group improvisation or the foundation of a song.
00696035 Book/Online Audio $14.99

BASS LINES

by Matt Scharfglass

500 expertly written bass lines, riffs and fills in a wide variety of musical genres are included in this comprehensive collection to help players expand their bass vocabulary. The examples cover many tempos, keys and feels, and include easy bass lines for beginners on up to advanced riffs for more experienced bassists.
00148194 Book/Online Audio $19.99

BLUES BASS

by Ed Friedland

Learn to play studying the songs of B.B. King, Stevie Ray Vaughan, Muddy Waters, Albert King, the Allman Brothers, T-Bone Walker, and many more. Learn riffs from blues classics including: Born Under a Bad Sign • Hideaway • Hoochie Coochie Man • Killing Floor • Pride and Joy • Sweet Home Chicago • The Thrill Is Gone • and more.
00695870 Book/Online Audio $14.99

COUNTRY BASS

by Glenn Letsch

21 songs, including: Act Naturally • Boot Scootin' Boogie • Crazy • Honky Tonk Man • Love You Out Loud • Luckenbach, Texas (Back to the Basics of Love) • No One Else on Earth • Ring of Fire • Southern Nights • Streets of Bakersfield • Whose Bed Have Your Boots Been Under? • and more.
00695928 Book/Online Audio $17.99

FRETLESS BASS

by Chris Kringel

18 songs, including: Bad Love • Continuum • Even Flow • Everytime You Go Away • Hocus Pocus • I Could Die for You • Jelly Roll • King of Pain • Kiss of Life • Lady in Red • Tears in Heaven • Very Early • What I Am • White Room • more.
00695850 .... $19.99

FUNK BASS

by Chris Kringel

This is your complete guide to learning the basics of grooving and soloing funk bass. Songs include: Can't Stop • I'll Take You There • Let's Groove • Stay • What Is Hip • and more.
00695792 Book/Online Audio $22.99

R&B BASS

by Glenn Letsch

This book/audio pack uses actual classic R&B, Motown, soul and funk songs to teach you how to groove in the style of James Jamerson, Bootsy Collins, Bob Babbitt, and many others. The 19 songs include: For Once in My Life • Knock on Wood • Mustang Sally • Respect • Soul Man • Stand by Me • and more.
00695823 Book/Online Audio $17.99

ROCK BASS

by Sean Malone

This book/audio pack uses songs from a myriad of rock genres to teach the key elements of rock bass. Includes: Another One Bites the Dust • Beast of Burden • Money • Roxanne • Smells like Teen Spirit • and more.
00695801 Book/Online Audio $21.99

SUPPLEMENTARY SONGBOOKS

These great songbooks correlate with Books 1-3 of the *Hal Leonard Bass Method*, giving students great songs to play while they're still learning! The audio tracks include great accompaniment and demo tracks.

EASY POP BASS LINES

20 great songs that students in Book 1 can master. Includes: Come as You Are • Crossfire • Great Balls of Fire • Imagine • Surfin' U.S.A. • Takin' Care of Business • Wild Thing • and more.
00695810 Book Only $9.99
00695809 Book/Online Audio $15.99

MORE EASY POP BASS LINES

20 great songs for Level 2 students. Includes: Bad, Bad Leroy Brown • Crazy Train • I Heard It Through the Grapevine • My Generation • Pride and Joy • Ramblin' Man • Summer of '69 • and more.
00695819 Book Only $12.99
00695818 Book/Online Audio $16.99

EVEN MORE EASY POP BASS LINES

20 great songs for Level 3 students, including: ABC • Another One Bites the Dust • Brick House • Come Together • Higher Ground • Iron Man • The Joker • Sweet Emotion • Under Pressure • more.
00695821 Book $9.99
00695820 Book/Online Audio $16.99

Visit Hal Leonard online at
www.halleonard.com

BASS BUILDERS

A series of technique book/audio packages created for the purposeful building and development of your chops. Each volume is written by an expert in that particular technique. And with the inclusion of audio, the added dimension of hearing exactly how to play particular grooves and techniques make these truly like private lessons.

BASS FOR BEGINNERS
by Glenn Letsch
00695099 Book/CD Pack........................ $19.95

BASS GROOVES
by Jon Liebman
00696028 Book/Online Audio $19.99

BASS IMPROVISATION
by Ed Friedland
00695164 Book/Online Audio $19.99

BLUES BASS
by Jon Liebman
00695235 Book/Online Audio $19.99

BUILDING WALKING BASS LINES
by Ed Friedland
00695008 Book/Online Audio $19.99

**RON CARTER –
BUILDING JAZZ BASS LINES**
00841240 Book/Online Audio $19.99

DICTIONARY OF BASS GROOVES
by Sean Malone
00695266 Book/Online Audio $14.95

EXPANDING WALKING BASS LINES
by Ed Friedland
00695026 Book/Online Audio $19.99

FINGERBOARD HARMONY FOR BASS
by Gary Willis
00695043 Book/Online Audio $17.99

FUNK BASS
by Jon Liebman
00699348 Book/Online Audio $19.99

FUNK/FUSION BASS
by Jon Liebman
00696553 Book/Online Audio $24.99

HIP-HOP BASS
by Josquin des Prés
00695589 Book/Online Audio $15.99

JAZZ BASS
by Ed Friedland
00695084 Book/Online Audio $17.99

**JERRY JEMMOTT –
BLUES AND RHYTHM &
BLUES BASS TECHNIQUE**
00695176 Book/CD Pack........................ $24.99

JUMP 'N' BLUES BASS
by Keith Rosier
00695292 Book/Online Audio $17.99

THE LOST ART OF COUNTRY BASS
by Keith Rosier
00695107 Book/Online Audio $19.99

PENTATONIC SCALES FOR BASS
by Ed Friedland
00696224 Book/Online Audio $19.99

REGGAE BASS
by Ed Friedland
00695163 Book/Online Audio $16.99

'70S FUNK & DISCO BASS
by Josquin des Prés
00695614 Book/Online Audio $16.99

**SIMPLIFIED SIGHT-READING
FOR BASS**
by Josquin des Prés
00695085 Book/Online Audio $17.99

6-STRING BASSICS
by David Gross
00695221 Book/Online Audio $14.99

HAL•LEONARD®

halleonard.com

Prices, contents and availability subject to change without notice; All prices are listed in U.S. funds